"*The Value* [illegible] ntial read for any employer. Ha [illegible] not just a process but a pivotal [illegible] tions, empowering people and driving profitability. Packed with practical advice and thought-provoking ideas, this book will change how you view payroll's role in your business success."

— Fiona Macintosh, Director,
More than Motivation Ltd

"This book is a must-read for every business owner who would like to improve functioning of their business. It provides an insightful exploration of payroll process and its impact on employers, employees and the entire organisation, offering practical tools for understanding and navigating pay-related challenges."

— Monika Jesorska, Payroll Administrator,
Chanonry Payroll Solutions Ltd

"This book is very well written. Not only does it make a wide-ranging and often complex topic understandable, it also champions the value that running compliant and efficient payroll can add to any business. This book is a must-read for any business owner, accountant or manager."

— Ian Bryceland, Director,
Ness Business Consulting Limited

"*The Value of Payroll* contains valuable insights for business in general. I very much enjoyed how the link was made to the payroll function. It has opened my eyes to the wider benefits of a well-run payroll within the business. Its content will be equally valuable to novice payroll, experienced payroll professionals, managers and directors alike. It may also be very beneficial setting the record straight and clarifying those myths and preconceptions around the constant changes new legislation brings with each new budget and each new government!"

— Lorna Clark, Director,
Genny Hire Ltd

"The book offers a comprehensive and well-structured guide to the value of payroll, at both a strategic and an operational level. It is an invaluable resource for business owners, HR professionals and payroll administrators. Written in a friendly and easy-to-understand style, it breaks down complex topics and offers insights into how payroll is integral to supporting long-term business goals through organisational efficiency and employee satisfaction."

— Alison Paton, Director,
Align People HR Limited

THE VALUE OF PAYROLL

TURNING
YOUR
BIGGEST COST
INTO YOUR
BIGGEST
ASSET

HAYLEY PATERSON

Cover image by: Salman Sarwar (99D)
Book design by: SWATT Books Ltd
Editing and proofreading: Craig Smith (CRS Editorial)

Printed in the United Kingdom
First Printing, 2025

ISBN: 978-1-0684476-0-0 (Paperback)
ISBN: 978-1-0684476-1-7 (eBook)

Hayley Paterson
Fortrose Scotland

www.thepayrollguide.co.uk

Contents

To my husband, Michael:

You're a never-ending support and encouragement to me. Your unwavering belief in me, and what I'm capable of, never ceases to amaze me. It's given me the courage to start my business and to be where I am today. Thank you for listening to my payroll ramblings.

To my son, Alfie:

You are the reason I started on the adventure of owning my own business. Without you, I wouldn't be where I am today. Thank you. I love you from your toes, to your nose, to where your hair grows, and everything in between.

To all my early readers, my book mentor, Karen, and those who shared their thoughts with me, to those who've supported me on LinkedIn – your contributions, inspiration and support have helped shape this book and me. Thank you.

Foreword

The Value of Payroll is a must-read for business owners, payroll professionals and HR or finance leaders who wish to deepen their understanding of payroll's vital role in organisational success. This book is a compelling exploration of the unseen efforts, complexities and strategic value of payroll, challenging the traditional perception of it as a mere operational cost.

Key Insights

Hayley dives into the intricate processes and compliance requirements that payroll professionals navigate daily. From tax regulations and employment law to case law precedents and audit readiness, the book sheds light on the immense expertise and precision required to ensure employees receive accurate payslips.

Through her personal experiences and anecdotes, Hayley reveals the emotional weight payroll professionals often carry. Mistakes are rare but deeply impactful, with even small errors causing significant stress. The book does a fantastic job of articulating how payroll professionals ensure compliance, maintain trust and avoid costly errors – all while remaining largely unnoticed unless something goes wrong.

A standout element is Hayley's ability to make complex topics accessible. Whether discussing the importance of rigorous documentation or how payroll contributes to risk management, she presents her insights with clarity and relevance.

Why This Book Matters

For business owners, *The Value of Payroll* is an eye-opener. It illustrates how payroll affects not only compliance but also employee trust and the financial health of a business. For payroll professionals, it offers validation of their hard work and a framework for advocating the importance of their role. HR and finance leaders will appreciate its focus on communication, transparency, and aligning payroll with broader organisational strategies.

Final Thoughts

Hayley's passion for payroll is evident throughout *The Value of Payroll*. Her dedication to highlighting the profession's importance, coupled with actionable insights and real-life examples, make this book an invaluable resource. It challenges readers to rethink payroll's role in their organisations, transforming it from a back-office necessity to a strategic enabler of success.

Whether you're managing a payroll team, overseeing compliance, or simply looking to better understand this crucial function, Hayley's book will leave you inspired and informed about the true value of payroll.

Kay Augustus MCIPPdip, CEO and Founder,
Augustus Payroll Services

CHAPTER 1

Introduction

Employer's great role,
Building lives, growth and purpose,
Payroll binds the goal.

Becoming an employer is one of the most significant responsibilities you can undertake. It's not just about filling a position in your business; it's about stepping into a role of influence over someone's livelihood. When you hire an employee, you're not only shaping their financial stability and career trajectory, but also playing a part in their sense of purpose. A single misstep in hiring can impact not just your business, but the life of someone who has entrusted you with their future. The stakes are high, and the ripple effects of a bad decision extend far beyond your bottom line, touching lives in ways you might not anticipate.

Hiring isn't simply about growing your business; it's about creating meaningful partnerships. Taking on an employee means offering more than a payslip; it's about providing opportunity, stability and a shared vision for the future. It requires careful preparation and a genuine commitment to helping others thrive. If you're not ready to approach this responsibility with integrity and purpose, it's better to hold off until you are. Being an employer means leading with accountability and recognising that the well-being of your team is closely tied to the success of your business. This isn't just a step for personal gain; it's about building something greater than yourself.

It's vital to recognise the dynamics between you and your employees. While your passion and drive fuel your business, your employees are there primarily for their own reasons - most importantly, to earn a living. They won't share your emotional investment in the business, nor should they be expected to. Their priorities and motivations may differ from yours, and that's okay. The key is to understand this dynamic and create an environment where their needs and contributions are respected. They don't work for you because you're nice (though it helps); they work because your business supports their goals, just as your employees and your business should support yours.

This is where a lot of business owners slip up. You can't assume your enthusiasm alone will be enough to motivate your team. You need to understand what drives them. What do they value? Is it financial security, opportunities for growth, work-life balance, or something else entirely? If you want your employees to stick around, perform well, and contribute meaningfully to your business, then you have to value what *they* value.

Remember, they're not there just for the journey; they're there for the destination, whether that's paying their bills, advancing their careers, or achieving their own personal goals. If you want to build a strong, motivated team, it starts with recognising that, while this business might be your dream, it's a job for them. Respect that reality and find ways to align their goals with the success of your business. When you do, you'll create a culture where everyone feels valued and invested, even if it's for different reasons.

Let's be honest, you didn't start your business on a whim. You did it for a reason. Maybe it's because you're passionate about what you do, and wanted the freedom to do it on your terms. Maybe it's about financial independence, having control over your time and your future. Or perhaps you've had a brilliant idea and want to make a real difference in people's lives, solving problems and creating something that matters. Whatever drove you to take the plunge, it's important to remember this: your responsibility isn't just to your employees, it's to yourself too.

What's the point of going through all the hard graft, navigating the highs and lows of entrepreneurship, if in the end, your own needs, or those of your family, aren't being met? Running a business is tough, it's demanding, and let's face it, it can be relentless. You deserve to benefit from your own hard work; to feel the freedom, fulfilment and success you set out to achieve. Yes, you have a duty to your employees, but that doesn't mean neglecting your own goals, well-being or quality of life.

It's about balance. It's about making sure that as you build something great for others, you're also building a life that works for you. If your business isn't helping you achieve that, then what's it all for? Never lose sight of the fact that you, too, are part of the equation. Make sure the reason you started your business stays front and centre.

Before we dive into the value payroll can bring to your business and how you can harness it to drive success, let me share a bit about my journey.

I've been working in payroll since 31st March 2003. Like the vast majority of payroll professionals, I didn't plan on it; it found me. After being made redundant from an office job, I attended my first jobseekers' meeting, where I enquired about a role. Little did I know, asking for details meant I had to apply for the job! Despite having no clue what the role involved, I applied, and got it. That job was a blend of payroll and purchase ledger, and that's where my payroll career began.

Five years later, I made the decision to focus fully on payroll and moved to my first payroll bureau. Since then, I've worked across a range of industries, in the oil and gas sector, and in various payroll bureaux, managing payrolls from one employee to over 8,000. On 1st March 2018, I launched my own payroll bureau.

I love payroll, not because it's easy - it isn't - but because I find great satisfaction in transforming something complex and stressful into something straightforward and manageable for both employers and their employees. It's incredibly rewarding to help people not only understand payroll, but take control of it. I'm passionate about helping and learning, and payroll gives me the chance to do both.

Many people think payroll is just about numbers, but it's so much more; it's about solving problems and working with people.

I founded my business out of necessity. After returning from maternity leave, I needed something that would provide the flexibility to continue my professional work, while allowing me to be there for my son. But it wasn't just flexibility that pushed me forward; my passion for payroll has been my driving force.

We handle outsourced payroll services at Chanonry Payroll Solutions Ltd, and we offer payroll consulting through our brand, The Payroll Guide, where we help employers and professionals with guidance on UK payroll. Having the two sides to the business allows me to support business owners no matter where they are on their employer journey, and what their needs may be, giving clients the flexibility to choose the solution that's right for them. Whether you want to hand over the processing of your payroll, or you're just starting as an employer and need guidance, my team and I are here to help. We also provide technical support to accountants, bookkeepers and HR consultants to help them support their own clients.

Throughout my years in payroll and through countless conversations with business owners, I've discovered that many of you don't fully understand what payroll entails, or your responsibilities. Most importantly, you don't realise how much value payroll can bring to your business.

Payroll often gets a bad reputation; it's seen as a cost, a burden, a necessary evil. It's tempting to avoid dealing with payroll, but then it becomes a bigger issue for you and your employees. Let's be honest, payroll wasn't the reason you started your business; it's just part of the deal. But when done right, payroll can deliver real benefits to your business - benefits that can positively impact your bottom line.

Yes, payroll is complex, and that's why its value is often overlooked. You can't sum it up in a simple sentence. Take marketing, for example. Good marketing drives sales, which boosts revenue - that's easy to grasp. The benefits of payroll are more subtle, but no less significant. Payroll professionals are constantly juggling tight deadlines, heavy workloads and a rapidly changing environment, making it challenging to convey the full value of payroll.

That's why I've written this book, to help you uncover the real value of payroll and how it can make running your business easier. Join me on this journey as I explore what payroll can truly do for you and your employees.

This isn't a how-to guide for running payroll or a deep dive into processing payslips. Instead, I'll uncover the hidden value payroll can bring to your business. Yes, I'll touch on the technical aspects along the way, but bear with me, as there's a purpose behind it all, and it just might change how you view payroll.

I've divided the book into three sections, focused on what I call the 3 Ps of payroll. Payroll touches on and influences three key areas of your business, which in turn influence payroll. These are:

Process
People
Profit

Let me take you through the 3 Ps of payroll and show you how to completely rethink your relationship with your payroll.

Process

First up is **Process**, the backbone of your business. Here, I'll cover everything from compliance and legislation, processes and procedures, to structure and control, and communication. These chapters explore how payroll affects the foundations of your business, and the systems that give it strength, stability and order. I'll wrap up this section with a chapter on the value payroll adds to your processes, digging deeper into how payroll not only supports but enhances your business operations.

People

Next, I move on to **People**, the heart of your business. In this section, I'll look at the role payroll plays in relation to your team, from different departments to employees, and even how it impacts marketing and sales, and your reputation. Your people are your business, and the way you manage payroll reflects on your employer brand. The final chapter in this section will bring together what I've discussed, showing how payroll plays a crucial role in nurturing your workforce and building a strong, loyal team.

Profit

Finally, I come to **Profit**, the lifeblood of your business. Just as blood sustains the body, profit is essential for growth, investment and fulfilling the vision you've set for your business. In this section, I'll walk you through understanding your numbers, assets, liabilities and your business' worth. Then, I'll tie it all together with a chapter on how payroll directly influences your profit, because the way you manage and perceive payroll can make or break your bottom line.

This journey through the 3 Ps of payroll will help you uncover the real, often overlooked, value payroll brings to your business. It's not just a cost; it's a vital component that, when managed well, can strengthen your foundations, inspire your people, and drive your profits. Are you ready to unlock that potential?

Ultimately, your payroll's value is determined by how much you choose to value it. If you see it only as an overhead, that's all it will ever be - an unavoidable cost. But if you treat it like the vital, strategic asset it is, you'll unlock its full potential. Payroll can help safeguard your business, streamline your operations and enhance your employee satisfaction, all of which contribute to long-term profitability and growth.

Remember, avoidance only feeds anxiety. Neglecting payroll will create problems that ripple through your entire business, from legal compliance issues to dissatisfied employees. By taking control of your payroll, you not only mitigate these risks but also open the door to new opportunities for business growth and success.

Payroll is not just about paying people; it's about realising the value it brings to your business. If you dedicate time and energy to improving your payroll process, your business will reap the rewards. By appreciating payroll for what it is - a crucial business asset - you'll be in a much stronger position to ensure compliance, boost employee morale and maximise profitability.

As mentioned, my aim with this book is not to educate you about payroll, though I hope you pick up some useful insights along the way. My goal is to shift your perspective; to make you see payroll in a completely different light. If you walk away from these pages thinking, *I've never thought about payroll like that before*, then this book has done exactly what I set out to do.

I want you to feel inspired to take action; to realise that payroll isn't just a necessary expense, it's a powerful tool that can drive your business forward. Now's the time to embrace that potential and make it work for you.

Each core chapter will explore a different area impacted by payroll. The final chapter in each section will tie everything together, showing how payroll can enhance your business through the lens of the 3 Ps.

Action points, to help you better understand your business and payroll, will end each chapter. I've created some handy templates and further info to help you complete these action points. You can download them from our website: www.thepayrollguide.co.uk

When payroll is managed effectively, it can deliver significant value to you and your business. If you value your people, your time and money, join me in discovering the value within your payroll. The future of your business depends on how you lead it today. Let's begin the journey towards lasting success. Now is the time to make payroll work for you, not against you, and take control of this vital aspect of your business.

Process

The journey of payroll from transactional to transformational marks a significant evolution in its role within a business, shifting from basic processing tasks to being a strategic function that drives business success.

Traditionally, payroll is seen as transactional, focusing on routine, repetitive tasks like entering hours, calculating wages, deductions and taxes, to ensure employees are paid accurately and on time. Payroll is often seen as a behind-the-scenes function; essential, yet unremarkable, with little impact on broader business strategy.

Over the years, payroll has strived for greater efficiency and accuracy, reducing the administrative burden and processing time, and minimising errors. With the advancement of technology and automation, software solutions have been developed to streamline payroll processes. These tools have allowed payroll teams to process faster and more accurately, while freeing up time that was spent on labour-intensive tasks to add more value.

As payroll systems evolved, they began to generate vast amounts of data and become engaged in more complex tasks. Businesses started to realise the potential of payroll data as a strategic asset, providing insights into workforce demographics and cost, productivity, absenteeism, and trends that could inform decision-making.

Payroll has moved on from simply processing data, to analysing it, helping businesses understand employee behaviour, optimise workforce costs and forecast financial outcomes.

Additionally, payroll has expanded beyond just paying employees, to enhancing their overall experience. Timely, accurate payroll directly impacts employee trust and satisfaction. Innovations, like flexible pay options, electronic and mobile payslips, and integrated time-tracking and attendance systems, have begun to transform payroll into a key contributor to employee engagement and financial wellness, aligning with broader HR strategies.

Payroll's role in compliance and risk management has become increasingly critical, especially as regulations around tax, pensions and employment law grow more complex. Payroll professionals now act as advisors, ensuring businesses stay compliant, avoid penalties, and manage risks effectively. This advisory role further highlights payroll's transformation from a transactional function to one that safeguards the business.

Today, payroll should be recognised as a strategic business partner. It plays a crucial role in workforce planning, financial forecasting and business strategy. Payroll professionals contribute insights that shape policies, drive efficiencies and enhance business performance. The transformational payroll function not only supports day-to-day operations, but also empowers your decision-making with data-driven strategies that align payroll with the goals of your business.

Payroll's journey to becoming a strategic partner has only just begun, in the eyes of many, but it has been developing for some time for those of us working in the profession. As technology continues to advance, payroll will further integrate into business ecosystems, becoming even more automated, accurate and strategic. This continuous transformation allows payroll to not only support, but also drive business innovation and growth.

The evolution from transactional to transformational reflects payroll's growing impact, shifting from a cost of doing business to a strategic enabler of success.

Over the next four chapters, I'll take you through some of the complexities of payroll in relation to processes and procedures within your business, providing some key aspects you need to be aware of. Then, in Chapter 6, I'll take you through how you can lean on payroll for support, and how payroll interacts with, and impacts on, your business processes and procedures, so that you can realise the value payroll can provide you and your business.

CHAPTER 2

Compliance and Legislation

Payroll's careful hand,
Guided by laws, firm and clear,
Keeps the business strong.

Safe to say, it's essential to stay on top of your business' compliance and legal obligations.

- Missing deadlines leads to penalties.
- Delayed payments to regulatory bodies will result in interest charges.
- Ignoring employment law can land you in court or on a public 'name and shame' list.
- Failure to pay your employees correctly and on time will result in a demotivated workforce that's both unproductive and unprofitable.

Neglecting these obligations can be costly, not just in terms of fines, penalties and interest, but also in terms of damaging your reputation, which can jeopardise your business' growth, stability and profitability. The UK's regulatory and legal landscape is complex, making it difficult for you to stay compliant.

Compliance and legislation are the foundations of employing staff and managing payroll. It's crucial to remember that, as the employer, the responsibility for compliance ultimately rests with you. It's your duty to ensure your business operates within the law. It's not optional. I strongly recommend having a payroll professional by your side to help you navigate the complexities and keep things running smoothly.

In this chapter, I'll give you an overview of some key points, as you need to grasp the principles before diving into the processes. Keep in mind, this isn't an exhaustive list. Compliance touches every corner of payroll and covering it all would be overwhelming. Instead, we'll focus on the main elements of compliance and legislation, giving you a clear sense of the complexities involved and how payroll plays a vital role in the structure and stability of your business.

While you don't need to master every detail, having a general understanding of the key aspects is required. This knowledge helps you identify when to seek advice, or take action, recognising and preventing potential issues before they arise.

Employment law is vast and continuously evolving due to new court rulings and shifts in the employment landscape. What's presented here, and throughout the rest of this book, is accurate at the date of publication. However, if these topics are relevant to your business, be sure to seek the most current information to stay fully compliant.

Adherence to Employment Law

UK employment laws are governed by key legislation, including the Employment Rights Act 1996[01] and the Working Time Regulations 1998[02], which contribute to establishing comprehensive standards for various aspects of employment. The Employment Rights Act consolidates laws on issues such as unfair dismissal, redundancy payments, wage protection and parental leave, while the Working Time Regulations provide essential rights regarding working hours, rest breaks and pay entitlements. Together, these laws help define the terms of employment, ensuring fair treatment and protection for employees, while setting clear legal boundaries for employers.

In the UK, laws addressing age, gender and ethnicity discrimination are primarily governed by the Equality Act 2010[03], which consolidates previous anti-discrimination laws into a single framework. This framework covers all aspects of discrimination in employment, including recruitment, terms of employment, promotion and dismissal. The Equality and Human Rights Commission (EHRC), established by the Equality Act 2006, enforces this legislation, providing a mechanism for employees to seek redress from their employers through employment tribunals. Tribunals have the authority to award compensation, and other remedies, when discrimination is proven.

Payroll navigates the complex maze of all this legislation to determine the correct actions to take in paying employees.

Tax Compliance

Payroll plays a critical role in tax compliance, particularly in handling deductions for PAYE (Pay As You Earn), income tax and NICs (National Insurance Contributions). Acting as a collection agent for the government, employers collect taxes from their employees through payroll, and remit them to HMRC, thereby reducing the administrative burden on the governing authority.

The introduction of RTI (Real Time Information) in April 2013 enhanced the efficiency of PAYE submissions, by requiring employers to submit tax information on or before each payday, rather than just at the end of the tax year. This system provides HMRC with more timely updates, improving the accuracy of tax payments and reducing discrepancies caused by incorrect tax codes.

Holiday and Leave Management

This issue has been a significant challenge for business owners for years, particularly in recent times, as maintaining compliance has become increasingly difficult. The landmark case, Harpur Trust v Brazel[04], brought this to the fore, dramatically changing payroll processes for calculating holiday entitlement and pay for ad hoc and part-year workers. The case began in 2019 when Lesley Brazel successfully claimed against her employer, Harpur Trust, in court, over underpaid holiday pay. The ruling caused widespread confusion regarding holiday pay entitlement for zero-hour and part-year workers, as the previously common practice of using the 12.07% method was ruled unlawful under the Working Time Directive 2003.

This method, previously documented as the calculation to use by HMRC and ACAS (the Advisory, Conciliation and Arbitration Service), had been the standard guidance for employers.

Following the ruling, both HMRC and ACAS quickly removed references to the 12.07% method from their websites, but failed to provide alternative guidance, leaving UK employers and payroll professionals frustrated and uncertain.

Harpur Trust appealed the ruling, which was reviewed in 2022, but the original decision was upheld. The court determined that holiday entitlement for these types of workers should match that of full-time employees, based on length of service, rather than hours worked. Although I won't delve into the specifics of the legal proceedings, this case underscores the critical impact case law can have on payroll practices, regulations and, ultimately, your business' financial health. It highlights that the legal duty of ensuring that pay is processed correctly belongs to the employer, so careful consideration of employment law is necessary when making decisions.

I had a new client with an ad hoc worker who was on the payroll all year round, but only worked a few times a year, 40 hours a week when needed. Despite working only sporadically, and only a few times a year, this employee was entitled to the full annual holiday allowance of 28 days. When calculating holiday pay based on their 52-week average, the employee's average weekly earnings were based on the 40 hours per week they worked during active periods. As a result, for one day of holiday, the employee was entitled to eight hours of pay. This resulted in the employee being entitled to more money for their holiday pay than for the actual hours they worked in that holiday year. While this is an extreme example, it illustrates the complexities employers face.

In response to the complex and costly position the Harpur Trust ruling had left employers in, new legislation, effective from 1st January 2024, reintroduced the 12.07% method and brought back rolled-up holiday pay, a method made illegal back in 2006. This change highlights the evolving nature of payroll regulations and the need to keep up to date with current legislation.

Calculating holiday entitlement and pay requires careful consideration of various factors, including the employee's contract type, working patterns, hours worked and when, and other elements like regular overtime and commission, as dictated by case law, and now the new holiday pay regulations. Due to the complexities of holiday calculations, payroll software struggles to assist with this task. The intricacies involved in payroll make it unlikely that technology will ever fully replace human expertise and experience in payroll processing, but the technological advances have greatly supported and will continue to support the payroll profession.

Accurate record-keeping and staying up to date with legislative changes are essential for managing holiday entitlement and pay. Although it demands significant time and resources, it is vital for ensuring compliance.

Contractual Compliance

It's a statutory requirement for every employee to receive written terms of employment. This not only protects the employee's rights but also safeguards your interests as the employer. A carefully constructed contract helps employers manage their workforce more effectively and ensures clarity on both parties' obligations.

Employment contracts must include legally required details and can be tailored to address business-specific needs.

Key areas to consider, along with the legal requirement, are:

- **Clarity and Expectations:** Clearly defined roles, responsibilities and performance standards reduce misunderstandings and ensure everyone knows what is expected of them, streamlining dispute resolution and keeping employees focused on their duties.

- **Legal Protection:** Contracts establish a legal framework that outlines the terms of employment, helping to protect employers during disputes, by providing a reference point for both parties.

- **Confidentiality and Non-compete Clauses:** Clauses protecting client confidentiality, intellectual property and business interests can be included, though enforcing non-compete clauses may be challenging and is under review.

- **Stability and Predictability:** Contracts typically specify notice periods, allowing employers time to find replacements. They also standardise key terms across the workforce while detailing any necessary variations.

- **Performance Standards and Dispute Resolution:** Employee handbooks, referenced in contracts, should outline performance and conduct standards, along with mechanisms for dispute resolution, such as arbitration or mediation, to avoid costly litigation.

- **Benefit Specifications and Holiday Entitlements:** Contracts should clearly outline remuneration, benefits and holiday entitlements. Provisions to reclaim items, like overpayments or unreturned business property, can also be included.

It's important to get the agreement with your employees right from day one. So, seek the advice of a trained and skilled HR professional who can guide you through the requirements and complexities of employee contracts, whilst safeguarding your business' interests.

Compliance with Pension Regulations

Pension auto-enrolment remains a significant administrative task for employers, despite its routine nature in payroll operations. Employers must adhere to strict regulations regarding employee eligibility, enrolment, reassessment and re-declaration of compliance every three years, ensuring ongoing conformance with The Pensions Regulator's requirements.

I was working in a payroll bureau as a Senior Payroll Administrator back in 2012, when pension auto-enrolment was introduced. It was introduced in stages, dependent on the size of business, with larger employers being required to set up first. We had clients of various size and structure. It was a huge undertaking getting all those employers' pensions set up on time.

Some employers set up early; others waited until the last minute. Employees needed to be assessed, and enrolled if they met the eligibility criteria. Clients were unsure what they needed to do, what they needed to set up, or about pensions in general. Some of our clients were already set up with pensions, but, back then, a pension was a good benefit to have, but it was normally larger employers that offered it, so the smaller clients struggled, especially with the additional cost.

I'm not a pensions advisor, but I often find myself being asked to explain pension auto-enrolment regulations and processes to clients. It's important to understand the process, your options, and know what you need to do, and when.

An example of the complexities involved can be seen during the re-assessment and re-declaration process. Employers must re-enrol eligible employees every three years, if they opted out 12 months or more ago. Effective communication and understanding of these regulations are essential to avoid misunderstandings and additional costs.

I was involved in a situation where a manager promised an employee a pension refund without understanding the regulatory process, leading to unnecessary complications.

The employer had just completed their re-assessment, and I had communicated with them several times ahead of this. One of their employees, who had opted out of the pension scheme over a year ago, was unhappy about being re-enrolled. He complained to his manager that he hadn't been notified about the pension deductions and demanded to be removed and refunded.

Without seeking advice, the manager apologised and promised the employee a refund, unaware of the regulations and the potential costs to the business. If the opt-out window had passed, the pension provider wouldn't refund the contributions, meaning the business would have to cover the cost. Additionally, as employee contributions receive tax relief, and if the employer covered the cost, a taxable benefit would be created, further increasing costs, so the employee's contributions would need to be amended to employer contributions to avoid this complication. The employee would keep their pension contributions for retirement. The promise was unnecessary and would cost the employer more than just the net value of the pension contributions.

A basic understanding of auto-enrolment rules, or knowing where to seek advice, along with better communication, would have avoided this risk and potential expense. I made sure the employee was given proper notice for future re-enrolment and explained the process clearly to all parties to prevent this from happening again. Safe to say, next time, the employee and employer won't be caught off guard!

Now, all ended well in this case. The employee followed the opt-out process through the pension provider, and it was within the opt-out window, so a full refund of the pension contribution was made. But with better handling, the process could have gone smoother. This illustrates one of the many ways that employers can cause themselves issues with compliance and legislation, if they don't understand the process.

By following the correct procedures, documenting them and maintaining clear communication, employers can prevent compliance issues and protect their business interests.

Benefits Administration

Managing employee benefits, like health and dental insurance or providing a company car, comes with strict regulations. The mandatory payrolling of benefits, planned from April 2026, brings a significant shift in how benefits are reported. While some benefits can already be payrolled, this change highlights the need for accurate tax and NIC handling. Employers must keep a tight grip on benefits administration to stay compliant and avoid fines.

Salary sacrifice schemes are another aspect to consider, as they offer a tax-efficient way for employees to enjoy benefits while saving on National Insurance. These schemes can be a win-win, helping employees reduce their taxable income while allowing employers to provide valuable perks. As with all benefits, maintaining strict control of administration and staying up to date with changes are crucial for compliance and avoiding penalties.

Statutory Payments

Statutory payments, like maternity, paternity and sick pay, are heavily regulated to protect employee entitlements and avoid discrimination. Employers must ensure accurate calculations, thorough record-keeping and adherence to regulations to remain compliant, address employee queries and be prepared for audits.

Minimum Wage Compliance

Payroll plays a critical role in ensuring compliance with NMW (National Minimum Wage) regulations. The NMW, along with the NLW (National Living Wage), currently for employees aged 21 and over, sets the minimum pay based on an employee's age. At the time of writing, the age at which the NLW kicks in is under review and is highly likely to be reduced in the future. For simplicity, both NMW and NLW will be referred to as NMW throughout this book.

It's vital to get the NMW right, not only to ensure fair compensation for your employees, but also to avoid hefty penalties. NMW rates typically increase every April, with significant rises in recent years, which contributes to the increasing cost of doing business.

The new NMW rate usually kicks in from the first pay period on or after 1st April. The same goes for when an employee moves into a higher age bracket – the new rate applies from the first pay period that begins on or after their birthday. Confusion often arises, with employees thinking the increase should happen on 1st April or on their actual birthday. Clear communication is key to avoid misunderstandings. Employers can raise wages at any time but aren't required to do so until the first pay period on or after the relevant date. If you do raise the rate early, make sure your employees know this, so you don't set expectations for future pay increases which you may not be in a position to accommodate.

Establish clear, upfront pay agreements that are fair across the business. It's common for some employees to feel they deserve more than they currently earn, and if you have an indispensable employee, their pay should reflect that. Regular communication, individual reviews and training can help ensure everyone is aware of pay rates and expectations. When making pay decisions, always consider the cost of recruiting and training new staff. Retaining current employees is often the more cost-effective recruitment strategy, rather than dealing with a high turnover.

I get emails from HMRC when they publish their list of employers who have breached NMW regulations – their 'name and shame' list. For instance, in February 2024, 524 businesses were publicly named, with employers ordered to repay nearly £16 million to over 172,000 employees, alongside additional financial penalties. Even large, well-known businesses made that list. A list you definitely want to avoid.

A common NMW violation involves employees' pay falling below the minimum when divided by the actual hours worked. This can happen for various, often innocent, reasons such as:

- Managers or employees failing to accurately report working hours.
- Lack of a robust system for tracking time worked.
- Misunderstandings about what counts as working time (e.g. time spent dressing in a required uniform or logging into systems before a shift).

Minor infractions that are quickly corrected, typically won't land a business on the NMW 'name and shame' list, but negligence or poor communication can easily land you in deep water. Once your business is listed, the reputational damage can be challenging to repair, or it can be permanent.

We'll discuss record-keeping in more detail a little later, but for now, maintaining accurate records of working hours is crucial for compliance. Without them, a business cannot prove it meets NMW obligations during an audit, and the burden of proof lies entirely with the employer. This is a common pitfall that leads many businesses to end up in trouble.

Audit and Inspection Readiness

Every business is subject to potential audits by HMRC and other regulatory bodies at any time. A compliant payroll process is essential for audit readiness, minimising the risk of negative outcomes and penalties. Additionally, it helps reduce the time, stress and resources required to navigate audits, allowing your team to remain focused on their core responsibilities.

Anti-fraud and Anti-money Laundering

Implementing rigorous checks and controls is essential to prevent payroll fraud, like the creation of ghost employees or unauthorised changes to payroll data. The importance of these measures is illustrated in the story below.

Several years ago, I began working as a Senior Payroll Administrator for a large company. There were eight of us in the Payroll department. Shortly after I joined, the business underwent an audit by HMRC, triggered by an employee's conversation with HMRC that uncovered a tax refund, processed and submitted for them, hadn't been paid to them. This led to the investigation by HMRC, revealing a significant fraud.

It was discovered that a former Payroll Supervisor, who had left before I started, had embezzled around £70,000 from the company over the course of around two years. The supervisor, who had isolated herself from the rest of the team, was given responsibility for processing one of the company's payrolls, with minimal oversight. Taking advantage of the lack of controls, she altered the bank details of employees due a tax refund, redirecting the funds to her own, or her husband's, bank accounts. Additionally, she used the records of employees who were set up in the system, but who never actually started working with the company, known as ghost employees, to make fraudulent payments to herself. The investigation revealed that she had committed similar frauds in her previous and subsequent roles with other employers.

Although I never met this individual, the story circulated that she used the stolen money for a deposit on a house and new boobs. She was eventually prosecuted and sentenced to prison for two years and four months for abusing a position of trust. Her husband, despite benefiting from the fraud, was not prosecuted. He claimed to know nothing about the fraud and went on to file for divorce. Unfortunately, their young child was left without their mother for some time, because of her actions.

This case highlights the critical need for structured processes, thorough checks and robust controls to protect your business from internal, as well as external, threats. Even in well-paying roles, like the one the Payroll Supervisor had, there are individuals who may not act in the best interest of the business. Therefore, safeguarding your employee's pay and sensitive information, through strict oversight, is paramount.

In addition, adherence to AML (Anti-Money Laundering) regulations is vital. Robust payroll procedures help prevent activities that could facilitate money laundering, and ensure that potential risks are swiftly identified and addressed, further securing your business against the risk of fraud.

Health and Safety Compliance

This may not be the first thing that comes to mind when considering payroll compliance, but health and safety plays a significant role in many businesses, with payroll often involved in key aspects. For example, certain legal requirements, such as providing health and safety training for specific professions, directly impact payroll. Employees must be compensated for the time spent on mandatory training related to their health and safety responsibilities. Failing to do so can lead to breaches of NMW regulations.

Payroll also intersects with health and safety through the reimbursement of expenses for items like PPE (Personal Protective Equipment), or specialised clothing required for employees' duties. Additionally, costs associated with health-related benefits, such as time off for eye exams, or reimbursements for prescription safety glasses, must be accurately tracked and recorded. Proper management of these elements is crucial, not only for staying compliant with health and safety laws, but also for controlling your business costs effectively.

Risk Management

The story I told on pages 37 and 38, about the Payroll Supervisor's embezzlement, underscores the significant risks associated with a poorly managed payroll process. Risks can range from reputational damage and deteriorating employee relations, to disruptions in business operations, all of which can impact on stability and profitability.

Structured processes with integrated controls help identify risks early, and errors can be corrected before they affect employees. This reduces the risk of financial loss and reputational damage. Moreover, a structured payroll process enables better planning and responses to potential disruptions, such as system failures, employee absences or unforeseen events, like a pandemic.

Performing a payroll risk assessment helps identify potential issues specific to your business, allowing for contingency planning and quicker, more efficient responses. It is crucial for businesses to have risk assessments done for health and safety in the workplace, to protect employees and visitors. A poorly managed payroll can be just as dangerous to your employees and your business, so performing a risk assessment for your payroll is just as important. This preparation not only mitigates risks, but alleviates the anxiety of potential payroll issues.

It takes away the worry and that 'what if?' feeling - the feeling of dread that lingers in the back of your mind when you think of all the things that can go wrong in your business. Through risk assessing, contingency planning, documenting, structure and control, you can rest easy, knowing you've thought things through, you've identified potential issues, and you know what to do if any of them come true.

In doing this, you'll be one step ahead of most business owners.

Payroll is seen as complicated, time-consuming, admin heavy and a necessary evil within business, and yes...it's all of this. It's easy to opt for the 'stick my head in the sand' approach, but avoidance breeds anxiety. If you manage payroll right, it can bring huge benefits to your business and relieve unnecessary stress by providing opportunities to mitigate against risks and, in turn, take control of your payroll process.

Reporting Requirements

Payroll is highly data-driven, requiring the collection and retention of various pieces of employee information and statistics. This includes tracking hours worked, sickness, holiday records and workforce costs associated with projects or products.

With the extensive data payroll manages, there are numerous reporting obligations. Regular submissions include the FPS (Full Payment Submission) to HMRC after each pay run, the EPS (Employer Payment Summary) to report adjustments to PAYE, and pension contribution reports to providers. Less frequent reports, such as P60s at tax year-end, are also crucial. Regardless of the frequency, all payroll reports must be accurate and timely, to maintain compliance and avoid penalties.

Penalties, Fines and Interest

Non-compliance with payroll regulations can result in penalties, fines and interest from regulatory bodies like HMRC and The Pensions Regulator. As already mentioned, non-compliance may lead to employee tribunals and court cases, resulting in legal costs and compensation payouts. Accurate, timely and compliant payroll processing is essential to mitigate these risks and protect your business from unnecessary financial losses, and reputational harm. Performing a risk assessment on your payroll can help you identify any areas of concern, and plan for reducing these risks, and the likelihood of compliance issues, which will help reduce the chances of you being non-compliant.

Data Protection Compliance

With the introduction of GDPR (the European Union's, General Data Protection Regulation)[05] on 25th May 2018, the emphasis on protecting personal data became clearer, and businesses were required to implement strict processes and procedures to safeguard this data. Although data protection was not new, GDPR reinforced the need for businesses to respect individuals' rights and handle personal data responsibly.

The ICO (Information Commissioner's Office) is charged with ensuring compliance to GDPR and the Data Protection Act 2018[06]. Certain businesses need to be registered with the ICO and pay an annual fee. The ICO has an easy-to-use online questionnaire you can go through, to find out if your business needs to be registered.

Payroll involves processing sensitive personal information, making GDPR compliance crucial. This requires the secure handling, storage and sharing of payroll data to protect it from misuse, and ensure the privacy of your employees.

What Does Compliance and Legislation Mean for Your Payroll?

Payroll compliance entails adhering to a complex web of regulations across taxation, employment law, benefits administration, data protection and more.

In many ways, payroll functions as the gatekeeper and information hub for compliance. Payroll safeguards the business from risks, by implementing robust processes, procedures and controls, coupled with effective communication. This not only ensures legal adherence, but also helps maintain your business' operations, protects its integrity, and creates trust among employees whilst avoiding costly penalties.

While compliance can be resource-intensive, demanding time and money, the cost of non-compliance is far greater. The potential damage to an employer's brand and reputation can be substantial; topics we'll explore in more detail in Chapters 9 and 10. However, when managed well, compliance can strengthen your business by demonstrating resilience, integrity, ethical operations and a commitment to both your employees and the broader community.

Start by identifying the legislation that affects your payroll, and ensure the relevant guidance is known and used within your business. This might seem overwhelming, and it's where a trained payroll professional comes in handy, to help you understand what aspects of compliance you need to know for your business and be a resource to keep you up to date with changes.

Main Points

- Neglecting your compliance and legal obligations can be costly, not just in terms of fines, penalties and interest, but also in damaging your reputation.
- Payroll regulations and employment law are vast and continuously evolving due to new court rulings and shifts in the employment landscape. Payroll plays a critical role in ensuring compliance.
- Accurate record-keeping and staying up to date with legislative changes are essential. Inadequate records undermine your ability to prove compliance with regulations, potentially leading to additional costs and reputational damage.
- Implementing rigorous checks and controls is essential to prevent payroll fraud, such as the creation of ghost employees or unauthorised changes to payroll data.
- A compliant payroll process is essential for audit readiness, minimising the risk of negative outcomes and penalties.

Action Points

- **Employee Contracts and Handbook:** Ensure every employee has a contract and your business has an up-to-date employee handbook.

- **Pension Procedure:** Review your pension process, ensuring compliance. Update letter templates and document the steps, including which letters to send and when, onboarding, offboarding and the three-year compliance re-declaration. Know your deadlines.

- **Compliance:** Identify relevant legislation for your business and payroll, and ensure everyone is informed. Set up regular checks for updates and understand new laws to ensure payroll is handled correctly from the start.

Chapter Endnotes

1 The National Archives, Legislation.gov.uk, Employment Rights Act 1996, last updated 4th January 2025: https://www.legislation.gov.uk/ukpga/1996/18/contents

2 The National Archives, Legislation.gov.uk, Working Time Regulations 1998, as viewed 6th January 2025: https://www.legislation.gov.uk/uksi/1998/1833/contents

3 The National Archives, Legislation.gov.uk, Equality Act 2010, last updated 4th January 2025: https://www.legislation.gov.uk/ukpga/2010/15/contents

4 The Supreme Court, Harpur Trust (Appellants) v Brazel (Respondent), last updated 16th April 2024: https://www.supremecourt.uk/cases/uksc-2019-0209

5 ICO (Information Commissioner's Office): https://ico.org.uk/for-organisations/uk-gdpr-guidance-and-resources/

6 The National Archives, Legislation.gov.uk, Data Protection Act 2018, last updated 11th January 2025: https://www.legislation.gov.uk/ukpga/2018/12/contents

CHAPTER 3

Processes and Procedures

Payroll's timely flow,
Streamlines tasks, sets order's pace,
Core to business growth.

In payroll, processes and procedures are as vital as location is in real estate – they're everything. And when those processes and procedures are well-documented and systemised, it not only protects your business from costly mistakes, but strengthens employee trust and ensures compliance.

In this chapter, we'll explore the crucial role that processes and procedures play in maintaining smooth, accurate payroll operations. Whether required by your business, HMRC or other third parties, these frameworks are essential for compliance, efficiency and ensuring employees are paid correctly and on time. I'll dive into the areas where these processes are indispensable, highlighting the importance of clarity and consistency in keeping your payroll running seamlessly.

By the end of this chapter, you'll understand how thorough documentation and regular reviews of your payroll processes are not just best practice, but a vital part of safeguarding your business from interruptions and inefficiencies. From onboarding new employees to dealing with audits and everything in between, I'll explain why clear procedures are the backbone of successful payroll management.

Every part of payroll, whether it's applying the correct tax codes, calculating pension contributions or dealing with statutory payments, relies on well-established processes. Without them, payroll operations can quickly unravel, leading to mistakes that impact employee trust, compliance and the smooth running of your business. In this chapter, we'll explore why these procedures are essential and why it's critical to document them thoroughly, review them regularly, and update them as payroll regulations evolve. Without this solid foundation, you risk errors that could harm both your employees and your business.

Documenting Payroll Procedures

You cannot document your payroll procedures enough. With frequent changes to payroll regulations and varying task frequencies, it's impossible to remember every detail. Comprehensive documentation, covering everything from pension uploads to year-end processing, is essential for smooth operations. Properly documented processes serve as a reference point for you and your team, helping avoid costly mistakes, especially in complex areas where employee circumstances or timing can change action points. In payroll, even small errors can lead to big problems, so detailed documentation helps keep everything running like clockwork.

Why Documentation Matters

Well-documented procedures are your business' insurance policy for payroll continuity. They ensure consistency, minimise errors and provide a clear guide if your payroll person is unavailable. Imagine your payroll administrator falls ill just before payday. Would anyone know how to carry on without them? Without proper documentation, your business could come to a grinding halt, employees might not be paid on time, and morale would plummet. Thorough documentation ensures that no matter what happens, payroll can be processed smoothly and accurately, keeping the business running and your employees satisfied.

Every aspect of payroll must be meticulously recorded and reported, whether it's hours worked, pension schedules or journal entries for accounts. These records are crucial for compliance, audits and business decision-making. Accurate reporting and record-keeping, supported by well-documented processes, enable informed decisions and ensure business continuity.

I'll speak more on the various interactions between payroll and other departments/groups of people within a business in Chapter 7. Communication (the topic of Chapter 5) and the flow of information help key personnel make the decisions they need to make for the business to keep moving forward and to support growth, but also, crucially, for the business to operate in a stable manner. Knowing your payroll cost projections enables good cash-flow forecasting (something we'll explore more in Chapter 12). This is all only possible with accurate, reliable and timely reporting and record-keeping, underpinned by strong and relevant processes and procedures, to know what information to gather, to keep data consistent, and to understand how and where to store the information.

Employers are legally required to keep detailed payroll records for the current tax year, plus the three previous tax years as per HMRC requirements. Records related to Covid-19 must be retained for at least six years, while certain payroll records classified as accountancy records need to be kept for seven years. These records must be accurate, comprehensive and readily available for audits, inspections and tribunal cases. Failure to produce the necessary records during a HMRC audit can result in penalties and further scrutiny. More importantly, inadequate records undermine your ability to prove compliance with regulations, potentially leading to additional costs and reputational damage.

I had a client, albeit briefly, that serves as a good example of this issue. We processed their payroll for only two months. After the first month, their sole employee resigned, so they were processed as a leaver in the second pay run. The employer decided not to hire a replacement, and we subsequently ceased their payroll with HMRC. Five months later, I was contacted by the employer, who told me that their former employee was taking them to a tribunal, claiming she had been underpaid for hours worked and holiday entitlement in her final pay.

The employer asked me to clarify the discrepancy. Was the payroll we processed correct, or was the employee's claim valid?

Unfortunately, my response wasn't what the employer had hoped for. I explained that the hours paid out in the final pay were based entirely on their instructions, and no breakdown was given. The client had told us the employee was due six days of holiday in her final pay. However, after further discussion with the employer at the time, it emerged that they hadn't set a defined holiday year for the business. In the absence of a designated holiday year, it defaults to the employee's start date. This meant the actual holiday entitlement was much higher; 19.2 days in total. The employee hadn't been paid for any holiday pay during their employment, so the full amount was paid out in their final pay, calculated based on information provided by the client. The employee claimed that the holiday hours paid were less than what her 52-week average hours determined using the record of hours worked that the employee had kept.

It was clear there had been a significant oversight and, regrettably, I wasn't able to offer much help beyond this. I haven't heard back from the employer, but given their lack of proper record-keeping and failure to comply with basic requirements, it was clear that if the case proceeded to tribunal, the employee would win. The employer would not only be liable for the additional sums owed, but could also face compensation claims and possible penalties for non-compliance, along with damage to their business' reputation.

This case highlights the importance of keeping accurate records, not just for your own management purposes, but to protect your business from potential legal and financial risks.

Key Areas to Document

Documenting payroll processes doesn't need to be complicated, but it does need to be thorough. Start by breaking down each step of the payroll process, from onboarding a new employee to handling leavers, making sure you include tax codes, deductions, pensions and pay dates. Write it all down in simple, clear language - this isn't the place for jargon.

Next, make sure you include key deadlines and responsibilities, so it's clear who's doing what and when. A flowchart can be handy for this, mapping out the process from start to finish. Then, store it somewhere accessible, where others can access it if you're unavailable.

Regularly review and update the documents, especially when regulations or business policies change. And don't forget to include backup procedures. For example, what happens if the payroll software crashes? Having documented payroll procedures means payroll can run smoothly, even if you're not around to oversee it.

Below are some key areas that require good documentation:

Onboarding and Offboarding: The process of bringing new employees into the business is critical. Properly documented onboarding ensures new hires are set up correctly from the get-go, with accurate tax codes, pension contributions and any relevant payments and deductions. Offboarding is just as important, ensuring final payments, holiday pay and deductions are handled properly, and P45s and pensions are processed in compliance with regulations. Without these processes in place, businesses risk costly pay errors and potential legal issues.

Managing Time and Attendance: Accurate payroll starts with precise time-tracking, especially for hourly employees. Clear procedures for collecting, verifying and processing timekeeping data, whether through paper timesheets, electronic systems or mobile apps, are essential to ensure payroll is accurate. Missteps here can lead to underpayment or overpayment, both of which can cause major headaches for you and your employees.

Payroll Policies: It's important to document business policies related to payroll, including holiday pay, sick leave, overtime and pay scales. Clear policies ensure everyone is on the same page, reducing the chances of errors or misunderstandings that can lead to inaccurate payments or compliance issues. Well-documented policies also create fairness and help maintain employee morale by ensuring consistency.

Payroll Software and Systems: Modern payroll systems handle vast amounts of data and complex calculations, but their accuracy relies on correct input and regular maintenance. Even minor data-entry mistakes, such as an unchecked box or an incorrect tax code, can have significant consequences. Documenting how to use these systems correctly is essential to minimising errors and ensuring payroll runs smoothly.

Training and Support: Relying on one person to handle payroll is risky. If they are unavailable, payroll operations could falter, leading to missed or inaccurate payments. Comprehensive documentation and cross-training ensure that someone else can step in when needed, maintaining business continuity and reducing stress on individuals.

Audit and Review: Being ready for an audit at any time is crucial for all businesses. Detailed records and structured processes make it easier to provide the evidence needed during an audit. Without them, an audit can become a daunting task, and poor record-keeping could land your business in trouble with the authorities.

Systemisation - The Key to Resilient Payroll: Systemising your payroll operations removes guesswork, ensures consistency and makes your business more resilient to unforeseen disruptions. Whether it's an unexpected illness, an IT failure or a global event like Covid-19, having a well-documented and systemised payroll process ensures that your business can continue to operate, no matter what. It's about having a reliable framework that makes payroll run smoothly, even when the unexpected happens.

Additional Payroll Procedures: Beyond time-tracking, there are numerous other aspects of payroll that need careful documentation, such as calculating statutory payments or correcting payroll errors. Keeping these procedures updated and easy to follow is crucial to maintaining compliance and business stability.

Business Continuity and Payroll

Payroll is a critical component of business continuity. If a crisis strikes, whether it's a fire, a software crash or another disruption, you need to be sure payroll will still be processed. The Covid-19 pandemic exposed just how vulnerable many businesses were, as many struggled to keep payroll functioning during lockdowns. Learn from these lessons and be prepared for the unexpected by ensuring your payroll processes are well-documented and systemised.

To create a robust business continuity plan for payroll, you should follow these key steps:

1. **Identify Potential Risks:** Start by assessing the types of disruptions that could impact payroll, such as IT failures, natural disasters, key personnel sickness or death, or staff shortages. Understanding these risks helps you plan more effectively. You can use the 'Payroll Risk Assessment' action point at the end of Chapter 4.

2. **Document Payroll Procedures:** Ensure that every aspect of your payroll process is thoroughly documented, from inputting data to processing payments. This should include backup procedures for key systems, software and data storage.

3. **Create a Backup Team:** Train a group of staff members who can take over payroll duties if your regular payroll team is unavailable. Cross-training ensures there are no single points of failure.

4. **Use Cloud-based Payroll Systems:** Consider using cloud-based payroll software that allows your team to process payroll remotely, if access to your office is restricted. This also provides automatic data backups.

5. **Test the Plan:** Regularly run payroll continuity tests to ensure your systems and team are ready for a potential disruption. This can highlight any gaps in your plan and give you the opportunity to address them.

6. **Establish Vendor Contacts:** Make sure you have up-to-date contact information for key vendors, such as your payroll software provider, so you can quickly resolve any technical issues during a crisis.

7. **Review and Update the Plan:** A business continuity plan should be a living document. Periodically review and update it to reflect changes in your business, staff or technology.

By following these steps, you'll be better prepared to keep your payroll running smoothly, even in times of disruption.

Continuous Improvement

Payroll processes are not static, they must evolve as regulations change, business structures shift, and technology advances. Regularly reviewing and improving your payroll procedures will ensure they remain robust, accurate and capable of supporting your business' future success. A simple process improvement might only save a few minutes of time, but these minutes can add up, and that little improvement could save extra time and money by reducing the potential for error. By focusing on continual improvement, your payroll operations will not only meet today's demands but will be ready for whatever tomorrow brings.

Main Points

- Every part of payroll, whether it's applying the correct tax codes, calculating pension contributions or dealing with statutory payments, relies on well-established processes.
- Well-documented procedures are your business' insurance policy for payroll continuity.
- Regularly review and update the documents, especially when regulations or business policies change.
- Clear policies ensure everyone is on the same page, reducing the chances of errors or misunderstandings that can lead to inaccurate payments or compliance issues.
- Systemising your payroll operations removes guesswork, ensures consistency and makes your business more resilient to unforeseen disruptions.

Action Points

- **Document Payroll Procedures:** Review and document every payroll task to ensure clarity and smoother processing.
- **Payroll Records:** Identify the records that need keeping, how long for, and ensure they're properly maintained, with access limited to authorised staff.
- **Business Continuity Plan:** Create a plan for payroll issues. Identify key personnel, knowledge and processes, ensuring others are trained and documentation is clear to handle tasks, if needed. Consider scenarios like office inaccessibility or payroll staff being unavailable.
- **Improvement:** Pinpoint areas needing improvement in payroll, starting with the most time-consuming or error-prone tasks, and develop a plan to streamline and enhance them.

CHAPTER 4

Structure and Control

Payroll's steady frame,
With controls, it guards the way,
Business finds its strength.

A well-structured payroll process with solid controls isn't just a 'nice to have', it's the skeletal structure of a smooth-running business. Think about it: payroll touches every employee, and even the smallest mistake can have far-reaching consequences, from compliance issues and financial penalties to damaged trust and lowered morale. A payroll system built on structure and robust controls ensures more than just accuracy; it guarantees efficiency, security and consistency. It provides accountability at every step and the scalability needed for growth, all while minimising the risk of costly errors. Ultimately, this framework not only keeps your business compliant, but also helps create trust and loyalty among your workforce.

In this chapter, we'll take a closer look at why implementing structure and control in payroll is vital for your business. I'll discuss how these elements not only safeguard your operations from risks but also contribute to creating a reliable and resilient payroll process. From reducing errors to enhancing transparency, a well-managed payroll can be a game-changer, both for your business' bottom line and your employees' confidence. Let's dive into the key reasons and tangible benefits that structure and control can bring, and how they can transform your payroll from a routine task into a strategic advantage.

Accuracy and Consistency

A standardised payroll process ensures that every step, from data collection to payslip distribution, is executed consistently. This reduces the likelihood of errors and ensures that all employees are paid accurately and on time. By maintaining consistency, data interpretation becomes easier, quicker and more reliable, which reduces errors and the resources needed for processing the payroll.

Built-in checkpoints and controls include:

- **Automated validation rules** that cross-check employee National Insurance letters, age increases for NMW and pension-age thresholds against predefined parameters.

- **Monthly payroll reviews**, where managers sign off on payroll reports before final submission.

- **System alerts**, such as for missing or incorrect National Insurance numbers or payment details.

- **Reconciliations** to identify discrepancies between recorded hours, pay elements and the data inputted into the payroll software.

- **Regular audits** to check procedures are being followed, and relevant documentation and records are being maintained.

Along with other checkpoints and controls throughout the payroll process, using the above ensures data accuracy. Such things help verify the accuracy of payroll calculations and records, promptly identifying and correcting any discrepancies. We will look at controls and checks in more detail in Chapter 6.

Compliance with Regulations

Structured processes and strong controls help ensure payroll operations comply with relevant employment laws and regulations, as discussed in Chapter 2. Proper checkpoints and data reconciliations, like those mentioned above, reduce the risk of legal issues, penalties and damage to your business' reputation.

Checks and controls also provide accountability for payroll personnel, minimising errors and the potential for fraud, as illustrated by Chapter 2's story about the Payroll Supervisor who embezzled. Additionally, maintaining detailed records and a clear payroll structure simplifies audits and inspections by regulatory bodies, such as HMRC.

Security and Confidentiality

Structured processes with strict access controls protect employee data from unauthorised access, preventing breaches.

Given the potential for fraud and embezzlement, it's vital to have controls in place that hold those who have access accountable and ensure no one operates unchecked. This safeguards employee information and the business' finances.

Efficiency and Productivity

A well-structured payroll process enhances operational efficiency. The increasing use of automation in payroll, supported by reliable software, streamlines processes, reduces processing time and minimises human error.

Employee Relationships – Trust and Satisfaction

Meeting payroll deadlines is crucial for employee trust and satisfaction. Consistent and accurate payroll processes ensure that employees are paid correctly and on time, which improves morale and productivity.

In Chapter 5, I'll explore how effective communication is vital to payroll success, but for now, note that structured processes provide a clear framework for payroll-related communication (internal and external), helping to build trust.

Continuous Improvement

Payroll is a dynamic process that requires ongoing adaptation to technological advancements and regulatory adaptations to support changes in the way people live and work. A structured approach allows for regular monitoring and assessment, facilitating continuous improvement and the implementation of best practices. Collecting feedback from payroll, employees and management enables your business to refine its processes over time to best fit the way you work, and to keep pace with growth and development.

Cost Management

Effective controls in payroll help manage costs by preventing overpayments, unauthorised processing and other financial discrepancies. This contributes to better financial management (the topic of Chapter 12), budgeting and overall control of payroll costs; one of the most significant expenses in any business.

Essential Payroll Controls

To enhance the accuracy, security and efficiency of your payroll processes, and minimise your payroll risks, consider implementing the following controls:

- **Checklists:** Ensure all tasks are completed and done consistently.
- **Segregation of Duties:** Separate payroll preparation, authorisation and distribution to prevent fraud and errors.
- **Access Controls:** Limit payroll system access to authorised personnel only.
- **Regular Reviews:** Regularly review system outputs and reports for accuracy.
- **Audits:** Conduct internal and external audits to verify compliance and efficiency.
- **Reconciliations:** Regularly reconcile data to ensure accuracy.
- **Automation:** Use reliable software to automate calculations and reduce manual errors.
- **Timekeeping:** Implement automated systems and approval processes for accurate timekeeping and timely payroll processing. Use tools like a payroll timeline and payroll calendars to assist.
- **Employee Verification:** Regularly update employee data to prevent errors and fraud.
- **Policies:** Maintain and update payroll policies to ensure consistency.

- **Confidentiality Measures:** Encrypt and securely store payroll data.
- **Compliance Monitoring:** Stay up to date with regulatory changes to maintain compliance.
- **Backup and Recovery:** Implement regular data backups and a business continuity plan to eliminate disruption in your payroll process.
- **Fraud Detection Mechanisms:** Embed fraud detection controls within your payroll process, such as audit trails and second-person checks.
- **Training and Development:** Provide regular training to stay informed and compliant.

The above payroll controls are there to support you and your business, whilst protecting your employees and safeguarding your business finances. I'll look at some of the above points in more detail in Chapter 6. Risk assessing your payroll will help identify any potential issues and allow you to plan for them, alleviate them or reduce their risk level.

If you need support creating or implementing any of the above into your payroll process, get in touch with me.

Structure and Control in Your Payroll Process

Structure and control are not just operational necessities, but the cornerstones of a successful payroll process. Without them, payroll can become a source of frustration, inaccuracy and even a liability, jeopardising both the financial health of your business and the trust your employees place in you. By establishing clear processes and implementing effective controls, you maintain accuracy, compliance, security and efficiency at every stage of the payroll cycle.

These elements form the bedrock of a reliable payroll system, which not only reduces the risk of costly errors and penalties, but creates transparency and accountability. A well-structured payroll process can significantly boost employee morale, as staff know they can trust that their pay will be delivered accurately and on time. Moreover, strong controls help safeguard sensitive data, ensuring your business stays compliant with regulations and maintains the highest standards of security.

Ultimately, structure and control in payroll are about more than just ticking boxes; they are key to your business' long-term stability and growth. By investing in a robust payroll system, you are investing in the confidence and satisfaction of your employees, safeguarding your business' reputation and setting the stage for scalability as your business grows. With a solid foundation in place, your payroll function can transform from a basic administrative task into a powerful tool that supports operational success and employee trust.

Remember that structure and control are not static; they should evolve alongside your business. Regularly reviewing and refining your payroll processes ensure they continue to meet the demands of an ever-changing regulatory and economic landscape, while keeping your workforce engaged and confident in your business' ability to deliver.

Main Points

- Significant risks are associated with a poorly managed payroll process. Risks can range from reputational damage and deteriorating employee relations to disruptions in business operations; all of which can impact stability and profitability.
- A well-structured and standardised payroll process with robust controls is critical for ensuring accuracy, compliance, efficiency, consistency, security, accountability and scalability.
- Controls, such as regular audits, checks and reconciliations help verify the accuracy of payroll calculations, promptly identifying and correcting any discrepancies. Integrated controls help identify risks early, and errors can be corrected before they affect employees or your business.
- Payroll is a dynamic process that requires ongoing adaptation to technological advancements and regulatory changes, to support the evolution in the way we live and work. Continuous review of your controls and checks is essential.
- Effective controls in payroll help manage costs by preventing overpayments, unauthorised processing and other financial discrepancies, contributing to better financial management.

Action Points

- **Checks and Controls:** Create a list of checks (points in your payroll processes when payroll is to be checked and reviewed) using tools such as reconciliations, manager sign-offs, software validations and others that have been mentioned. Look at ways to alleviate the potential for fraud and errors, and help maintain accuracy and good record-keeping. Identify who should perform the checks and reviews.

- **Audit:** Perform an audit on your payroll. This could be an internal audit by someone not normally involved in the process, like yourself or a senior manager; or an external audit, whereby you bring in an external consultant to perform the audit. The auditor should ensure relevant processes are in place, documented and followed, with appropriate records securely maintained. They should also identify who has access to what information and assess the justification for that access.

- **Backup:** Create a payroll backup routine to safeguard against data loss or corruption. Identify what needs to be backed up, how often, where the backup should be stored and for how long.

- **Payroll Risk Assessment:** Using information from this and previous chapters, identify the areas that have potential for compliance issues, or other risks within your business. Then, document controls and procedures to mitigate against those risks, and identify and implement checks to maintain compliance. You can use my Payroll Risk Assessment template, available on www.thepayrollguide.co.uk to help you.

CHAPTER 5

Communication

Payroll's complex maze,
Communication lights the way,
Error-free, we stay.

Did you ever play Chinese whispers as a child? I remember it well from when I was young, and my son has played it recently at school. The goal of my son's class game is simple: if the word whispered around the circle remains intact, the kids get whatever the word was, like biscuits or ice cream. But as we know, the message often gets distorted, illustrating how easily communication can be misunderstood.

This game highlights a fundamental challenge in communication; it's prone to misinterpretation, leading to confusion and frustration. In the realm of payroll, this can create a disengaged and unproductive workforce, which can further damage your business' reputation, through negative word of mouth. Payroll is often a real-world example of Chinese whispers, where what actually happened, or the information you're trying to convey, often gets distorted and confused.

In this chapter, we'll dive into the critical role communication plays in the payroll process and its impact on your business. In payroll, errors and misunderstandings can lead to employee frustration, reduced engagement and even reputational damage. I emphasise the importance of clear, consistent and timely communication, outlining key aspects such as accessibility, transparency and the need for feedback loops. I also touch on the importance of educating employees about payroll and the consequences of poor communication, sharing cautionary tales that illustrate how easily things can go wrong when communication breaks down. Effective communication, especially in payroll, is crucial for maintaining trust, ensuring compliance, and creating a productive and harmonious workplace.

Communication is complex. I could write an entire book on it. However, to focus on the importance of communication in payroll, and its broader impact on your business, I've broken down the topic into 16 key aspects, each with specific relevance to payroll.

Clarity

Clear, concise and well-documented payroll information ensures that everyone understands the processes and procedures involved. It makes sure everyone is on the same page. Having a clear communication strategy for your payroll will keep your team informed, so they know what the different aspects of their pay mean, how they are calculated, what they need to do if something's not right, or they have a question. This reduces stress, speeds up issue resolution and saves time in payroll processing, ultimately benefiting your business.

Timeliness

Payroll operates to strict deadlines. Whether it's paying the employees, submitting the payroll data to HMRC or paying the pension contributions, whatever it is in payroll, the deadlines are not movable and must be met. If information isn't communicated clearly and promptly, inaccuracies and delays can occur, disrupting the entire payroll process and affecting other parts of the business too.

Consistency

Consistent communication ensures that everyone receives the same information simultaneously, reducing confusion and helping to meet deadlines. It also keeps things fair. One of the biggest distractions for employees is when they don't think they're being treated fairly. Fairness, through consistency, keeps employees motivated and productive.

Transparency

Transparency in payroll processes reassures employees that they are being treated fairly. It helps demonstrate what the process is, and why things are done that way, reducing misunderstandings and complaints.

Accessibility

Having easy access to payroll information minimises confusion and questions, saves time and allows employees to remain focused on their work. Accessibility is key to keep the process flowing and for completion of the task in a timely manner, with the least amount of fuss possible. Information is powerful, and having access to clear, concise and well-communicated information that helps employees understand their pay and benefits, ultimately benefits your business.

Feedback and Support

Communication is a two-way street. Listening to employee feedback helps to quickly resolve issues, whether from payroll answering a question or addressing a concern. Clear answers build trust and keep operations smooth. Supporting employees in understanding their pay and benefits makes a big difference in keeping things running efficiently.

When communication breaks down, frustration and mistrust can grow, making processing the payroll harder for everyone. Payroll relies on feedback to fix issues early, but tight deadlines often mean we're focused on getting through our workload. This is why we need your support as a business owner, and from employees. The better the information that is shared with payroll, the more efficiently we can work, and the more time we have to answer questions and communicate proactively.

Training and Education

Payroll literacy is crucial yet often overlooked in education. When I went to school, I had zero education on payroll and how I would be paid in the working world, and nothing much has changed since then. Young people get out of school and have very little knowledge of how to manage their money and how their pay is calculated, if they work for someone else. Even if you leave school and decide to go straight into being an entrepreneur, you still need to know about payroll, especially if you are a limited company and paying yourself as the director, or if you're going to hire a team to support you. This is something that really frustrates me, and will be the focus of my next book. I want to ensure young people are fully prepared and understand the processes.

But this doesn't just affect young people.

More emphasis needs to be put on this important part of everyone's life. Most employees we've supported in our payroll bureau, and through The Payroll Guide, don't know much about payroll, and we often need to teach them the basics before we can address their query. Often, their query is purely because they don't understand the processes and procedures, and this needs to change.

Policy

HR oversees several policies that directly impact payroll. The policies you need depend on your business size and type; some are set by law, others by your preferences as a business owner/ manager. Small businesses often have informal policies, but it's always best to document them and make them accessible to everyone.

Having policies is important, but the real value lies in communicating them clearly. This ensures everyone understands the processes, procedures and expectations, helping employees meet them. Even if a policy isn't legally required, it's a good idea to document how you want your business to run. This keeps everyone aligned and can make payroll smoother. A HR professional can guide you through this process.

Error Resolution

Payroll is complicated and relies on lots of different variables, and different people being involved, providing data. This inevitably means errors happen. Good processes and procedures can help reduce the likelihood of errors occurring, but there will always be some that sneak through. Payroll can never be 100% accurate - there are just too many variables.

When an error occurs, effective and timely communication is crucial to avoid loss of time, as well as frustration and stress building in those involved. You need to clearly let employees know what to do and who to speak to if they notice an error in their wages. It's important to give clear communication on what will happen and when the employee will get a response to their query/issue. Communicating the busy times for payroll is important, as there are certain times of the month that payroll is extremely busy, meaning response times will be affected. Communicating this to employees manages their expectations.

Confidentiality

There are so many opportunities in payroll where a personal data breach could happen. This is a big reason why your processes and procedures need to be strong. Careful consideration of how personal data is communicated, and to who, is needed to ensure the personal data is not given to someone who doesn't have a legitimate reason for receiving it.

We need to ensure that the software and automation used in payroll meets the required standards for confidentiality – that everyone involved in the payroll process is fully briefed on what is required of them, and the potential risks involved. Communication, through documented policies and procedures, for the use of personal data can assist in ensuring everyone knows what they need to do in different situations.

Compliance

I covered quite a bit on compliance in Chapter 2. Compliance is a lot to take in, and the tricky part is that the government is continuously changing and updating legislation and employer requirements. It is necessary for you to keep pace with the changing employment landscape, but it's difficult enough for us payroll professionals to keep up to date with it all, that employers often struggle. This is why I always recommend having a payroll professional at your disposal, to support you with this enormous task.

Non-compliance can cost...big. There are so many penalties, fees and interest charges associated with payroll. If you don't do what you need to do, when you need to do it, it's going to cost you.

So, you can see, strong communication and tight control of deadlines are essential to avoid these costly charges. But it's not just the penalties that make up the cost of poor communication; when it affects compliance, there's a cost to reputation too, which I'll speak more on in Chapter 10. Non-compliance has a huge impact on a business' reputation and, often, the cause comes down to miscommunication or lack thereof.

Change Management

Some people embrace it more than others, but let's be honest, nobody likes change. We fear the unknown, we feel like we're losing control and that it threatens our comfort zone. Personal factors, such as previous experience, might taint the proposed change; that, or poor communication.

In my experience, the factors that might affect someone's ability to accept change can be managed, to a certain extent. Any real issues normally come down to the way the change has been communicated, and the information and support provided during the transition period. This determines the employee's response to the change.

Payroll is constantly changing, and it needs to. From updates in legislation to making sure employees are treated fairly and that the appropriate taxes are paid, to updates in technology, assisting with the admin and manual burden of payroll, increasing efficiencies and saving on resources.

I've seen a fair few changes whilst working in the payroll profession; the introduction of RTI and pension auto-enrolment, to name a couple of the big ones. But there are many more that you might not be fully aware of, including some smaller tweaks, like to the Tips Bill – the Employment (Allocation of Tips) Act 2023[07] – to ensure employees receive the full amount of tips paid by clients. Others are more substantial, like the upheaval and changes to the holiday entitlement for ad hoc and part-year workers, as mentioned in Chapter 2.

The rate of change in payroll is growing. Every change in government, with new policy ideas and tax year changes, doesn't just come with new rates and thresholds to learn; they come with changes in employment law, process and procedural regulations, and increases in automation and online submission requirements, all making the change burden a big part of payroll. The volume of changes and the many different types of change can easily cause confusion, leading to errors and misunderstandings. Strong communication is critical here, but often communication is hampered by poor guidance from governmental bodies, leaving confusion and procedural questions for different scenarios. But the end responsibility for ensuring accuracy and compliance for your payroll, is yours, as the employer, so you must have an understanding of the requirements.

Cultural Sensitivity

The UK workforce is diverse, and that's what brings quality and variation within businesses. But with this diverse workforce come language barriers and cultural differences in communication styles. This means that payroll communication needs to be tailored to accommodate the different cultures. Good communication, designed to educate the masses, but tailored to the individual, will unite the team and support the business to reach its goals.

Employee Engagement

Communication is a tool to be used by businesses; something that can engage, unite the team and ultimately assist in retaining employees. Clear communication makes dealing with employees easier, it saves time, and it saves frustration from building. The more that your employees are frustrated and worried about their pay, the less they are focused on their work. So, use effective communication to engage your employees. It makes the working environment much more pleasant and your employees will be easier to manage for it.

Technology Utilisation

Leveraging technology helps streamline payroll communication, due to the abundance and variation of communication required. But it's important to identify what is relevant and works for your business and your employees. Every business and team are different, so what works for one, might not work so well for another. There will be some trial and error, and the best way to know how to communicate with your employees is to ask them.

Technology also plays a big part in the communication of payroll data to governing bodies, with the requirement to submit data online increasing substantially over the last 10 years. With the introduction of RTI by HMRC, the fate for payroll was sealed when it comes to the reliance on technology. Payroll information needs to be communicated to HMRC, pension providers and other third parties, electronically and regularly. Long gone are the days of handwritten P11 forms, where payroll manually calculated statutory deductions and employees' net pay.

Be warned though, technology can create a workforce focused on what to do, rather than why it's done. Payroll professionals must be skilled with technology but also understand the reasoning behind the calculations to ensure accuracy, and explain them clearly to employees and employers.

Coordination Between Departments

I'll delve into the interactions between departments and payroll later, in Chapter 7. But, for now, it's communication that holds up the relationships between departments, and the internal structure and functioning success of the business. If the flow of the right information, in the right format, and at the right time, doesn't occur, then the business cannot meet its objectives, and productivity, profitability and growth potential are decreased.

Tales of Caution – When Communication Breaks Down

I could tell numerous stories of what can happen when there's a lack of communication, or when communication is poor or ineffective. When communication breaks down, the consequences can be severe. I've encountered many situations where poor communication has led to frustration and stress. But with prompt, clear communication, even the most difficult situations can be resolved.

Unfortunately, most of the stories I could tell are not of a sunny disposition; they involve a lot of shouting and blame, often resulting in unhappy employees, and breakdowns in communication and trust. But the ones I've been involved in all had happy endings, as I helped the employer get everything sorted out, and let them know how to prevent it happening again. Most stories require a bit of background knowledge or are sensitive in nature, so, below, I'll mention a few quick examples to illustrate how a breakdown in communication can affect your business.

The first tale about poor communication leads to an angry employee, as these stories often do, and took place not long after I started at my first payroll bureau, just over five years into my payroll career. An employee of a client, who a colleague of mine processed, came into our reception area shouting and cursing, and wanting to speak to someone about his pay. My colleague didn't want to speak with the gentleman, which I understood; nobody wants to deal with an irate person. But someone needed to talk to him. That someone was me. Within five minutes I managed to calm him down enough to talk to me and tell me what the issue was. Another five minutes and I had talked him through what had happened, the reasons behind it, what everything meant, the implications of it, and what would happen to resolve it. The employee left with a thank you.

It took just 10 minutes of my time, my knowledge and experience, and more importantly direct communication - one-on-one - with the employee to resolve the tension and frustration that had built up in the employee.

Nobody wants to be an irate employee, but the complexities and the importance of payroll to employees often leads to strong outbursts like this. This incident has stuck with me through the years, and taught me a valuable lesson. When something goes wrong, communication needs to be swift and on a one-to-one basis with the person who has suffered the error. Quick and effective communication will hold back the frustration and stress, and give the employer time to rectify the issue. Mistakes happen and, due to the complexities, payroll is prone to them. It's our skills in communication that will ultimately affect the outcome and the ease at which the issue can be resolved.

The second story illustrates why DIY for payroll is not always the best idea, unless you have a guide. I quite often find an issue or two to resolve whilst going through the onboarding process with new clients for our outsource service. It may be that things have not been done quite right, or there are data record issues.

One new client came on board who had run their payroll themselves and had decided it was time to outsource, as it was getting a bit much for them. They had a number of new employees start with them over the previous six months and had failed to provide the new starters with pension letters, and failed to assess their employees for pension auto-enrolment.

Around half a dozen employees should have received postponement pension letters. As this important communication had not taken place, and these letters hadn't been provided to the employees within the first six weeks of their employment, this meant that the employer was no longer eligible to postpone those employees, and they needed to assess the employees for pension auto-enrolment from day one. They had all met the criteria for pension auto-enrolment, so needed to be put into the pension scheme. They then required their pension contributions to be backdated to when they first met the pension auto-enrolment criteria.

This caused an inconvenience to the employer to now rectify the issue, and to the employees who should have had pension contributions invested for them earlier. There was an additional cost to the employer, due to the lack of timely postponement letters, they lost the opportunity to postpone the employees, meaning more employer pension contributions were due, and time was wasted sorting out the issue. There were a few other data issues with this employer's records, all of which I sorted out.

Knowing all the procedures that need to be followed, the communications that need to be made, and when they need to be made, is difficult for employers to keep on top of. You've got enough on your plate, and that's why having a payroll professional to guide you, can take the weight off your mind.

There's so much to remember in payroll, such as different payment structures, variations in working patterns and payment components, meaning it's easy to miss things. When processing the payroll is not at the front of your mind, when it needs to be, and when you put off processing until the last minute, then it increases the chance of errors. You're busy, there are lots of plates you need to spin; I get that, I'm spinning the same plates myself. But to bury your head and not take the bull by the horns, and tackle your payroll, giving it the attention it needs and deserves, will only make processing your payroll more difficult, and more stressful for you. I've had clients leave things to the last minute and in a rush get their payroll data over to us late. This puts pressure on us to turn the payroll around, under tight timescales, and leaves us more open to error.

One client recently forgot to process tips for their employees as they'd been rushing to send over their data. Due to the lateness in the day, there was no time to correct the pay run, before payday. This affected the amount that the employees received; importantly, the money they had to pay their bills and afford their lives. Missed payments will be remembered by employees and can erode away the trust they have in you.

Then, there is unclear data, or provision of only part of the required information. This causes confusion and wasted time for us and the client, as we are required to question and request the additional information. It can only ever lead to processing errors and stress for all involved.

Common areas where this can happen are:

- **Holidays:** Not providing the dates the employee took off on holiday – we need this to be able to calculate the holiday payout and it acts as a record for the employer of what days have been taken. This is particularly important for ad hoc and part-year workers.

- **New Starters:** There's certain information that payroll requires to submit to HMRC and needs to determine the tax code or National Insurance letter that should be operated for the employee, which ultimately determines the employee's net pay.

- **Leavers:** We need an accurate last day for a leaver. This can determine things like their final pay amount and their holiday entitlement payout.

So, a wee plea from me: if your payroll person gives you a list of certain information they require to process your payroll, provide it in the most clear and concise manner you can. This will save you time and make your payroll process so much easier.

In payroll, communication is critical. Effective communication maintains accuracy, compliance, employee satisfaction, promotes efficiency within the payroll process and the operations of the business as a whole. It helps to prevent misunderstandings, wasted time, errors and legal issues. A well-functioning, transparent payroll through effective communication makes the running of your business easier.

Main Points

- Information that isn't communicated clearly and promptly results in errors and delays, disrupting the entire payroll process and affecting other parts of your business.

- Good communication, designed to educate the masses, but tailored to the individual, will unite the team and support the business to reach its goals.

- Payroll can't be 100% accurate; there are too many variables. Strong communication, processes and procedures help alleviate errors and support quick resolution when errors do occur.

- Payroll is such an important aspect of everyone's lives; it needs to be taught to young people leaving school, college or university, then throughout people's working lives, so everyone's fully prepared and understands the processes.

- The end responsibility for ensuring accuracy and compliance for your payroll is the employer's, so you must have an understanding of your requirements.

Action Points

- **Communication Strategy:** Develop and document a payroll communication plan. Identify what needs to be shared, who should deliver the message and the best communication style for clarity. Ask employees what info they want and how they prefer to receive it.

- **Feedback:** Set up a process for employees to give feedback and ask pay-related questions. Include regular engagements with them to understand frustrations and their suggestions for improving the payroll process, and take action on their ideas.

- **Policies:** Identify and document the essential employee policies for your business, including legal requirements and internal processes to support operations.

Chapter Endnote

7 The National Archives, Legislation.gov.uk, Employment (Allocation of Tips) Act 2023, as viewed 15th February 2025: https://www.legislation.gov.uk/ukpga/2023/13/contents

CHAPTER 6

The Value of Payroll to Process

Payroll's pulse sustains,
Business flows in harmony,
Efficiency thrives.

Processes and procedures are essential components of a business' operations and success. You can see they provide structure, consistency and efficiency, which are vital for achieving your business goals. Through processes and procedures you can gain a level of control over your business' operations. This control is essential. But it's not something you can achieve by yourself, nor should you try.

Don't panic if you've read through the previous chapters thinking there is so much more I should be doing, that I should know. Take it one step at a time. Reading this book will give you an overview of the things you need to consider, of the potential of payroll, and why you should value it. The expertise of a payroll professional adds real value to your business' processes.

In this chapter, I'll explore the critical role payroll data plays in driving your business forward. I'll take a deep dive into how processes and procedures have evolved over time, and how payroll has, and continues to, shape and influence business operations. I'll walk you through the key elements of processes and procedures, showing you the real value payroll can offer in streamlining and improving them. Then, I'll go a step further and examine how payroll can be used as a strategic tool in your business toolkit, with practical examples that demonstrate its impact.

As outlined at the beginning of the Process section, payroll has moved away from merely providing a transactional contribution to businesses. The introduction of technology and automation have allowed payroll the opportunity to gather data that is vital for strategic decision-making. The continual advancement of employment law, compliance, financial planning and employee satisfaction requirements have developed payroll further. This has allowed us to provide valuable services to businesses in areas such as:

- **Workforce Planning and Management:** Payroll data provides insights into workforce costs, overtime trends and staffing needs, helping you optimise scheduling and allocate resources efficiently. This enables better forecasting of workforce needs and reduces costs associated with overstaffing or understaffing.

- **Ensuring Compliance and Reducing Risk:** Payroll keeps employers in line with UK laws and regulations, like HMRC requirements, NICs and pension auto-enrolment. Keeping up with ever-changing tax codes, minimum wage increases and statutory requirements can be a headache. Payroll handle this, reducing the risk of non-compliance fines or costly legal disputes. Payroll take the stress off you, ensuring everything's handled correctly and on time.

- **RTI:** Since the introduction of RTI reporting to HMRC, payroll systems must now report every pay run. A robust payroll process ensures this happens without any disruption, keeping you on track with your legal obligations, while reducing the administrative burden.

- **Operational Efficiency:** Streamlining payroll processes through automation reduces the administrative burden and errors. This frees up time within the payroll team, allowing us to focus on strategic activities that can boost overall operational efficiency, and provides the resources to give an enhanced experience to employees.

- **Data-driven Decision-making:** Payroll data provides valuable insights into financial aspects such as cost per employee, productivity and ROI (Return On Investment) of the human element to your business. This informs strategic decisions related to items such as workforce restructuring, cost optimisation and long-term planning.

- **Talent Acquisition and Compensation Strategy:** Payroll data helps businesses develop competitive compensation packages that attract top talent, while aligning with budget constraints. This supports strategic hiring decisions and ensures compensation aligns with market standards, and provides better understanding of the impacts to the business' financial situation, now and into the future, with different compensation package options.

- **Streamlining Processes and Saving Time:** A well-run payroll system streamlines what could otherwise be a manual, time-consuming process. Automating payroll tasks means fewer human errors, faster processing and more time freed up for other important tasks for your payroll personnel, yourself, and others within the business. It's all about working smarter, not harder.

- **Strategic Alignment with Business Goals:** Payroll supports the alignment of compensation policies with the business' strategic goals, such as rewarding employee innovation or meeting their sales targets. This ensures that pay structures and incentive programmes directly contribute to achieving key business objectives, making sure the valuable financial resources of your business are allocated to areas that provide the most value to your business.

As you can see, payroll is a critical component to overall business operations and success. Let's take a step back for a moment and look at what payroll data is, and why it's important to your business and your decision-making.

Understanding Payroll Data

Payroll data supports a business, like the foundations of a house support the structure above. Just as strong foundations ensure the stability and safety of the entire building, accurate payroll data ensures the smooth operation of your business. It does this by providing crucial insights into workforce costs, employee productivity and your business' financial health.

Without solid foundations, the house would be unstable. Similarly, without reliable payroll data, a business would struggle with budgeting, compliance and strategic planning. Payroll data keeps the business grounded, enabling informed decision-making that supports growth and sustainability.

Payroll data refers to the information and records related to the compensation of employees within your business. This data encompasses a wide range of details that are essential to calculations, processing and managing employee's pay accurately, and in compliance with legal requirements.

Payroll data not only involves basic salary information, but incorporates various other components and factors that influence the operational and strategic success of your business, such as:

- employee information
- compensation details
- deductions and withholdings
- benefits data
- statutory payments and supporting information
- time and attendance records
- pay history
- holiday records
- compliance information.

Payroll data comes from various sources, both within the business and externally, and payroll's expertise lies in collecting, processing and recording this data accurately, which adds real value to your business.

Let's briefly explore how payroll data, along with its processes and procedures, supports key business functions.

Accurate and Timely Pay: Accuracy in payroll isn't optional; it's crucial. Employees must be paid correctly and on time. Key tools include checklists, reconciliations, payroll calendars and timelines.

Regulatory Compliance: Payroll ensures your business stays compliant with tax and employment laws. This is achieved through continuous staff development, clear communication and up-to-date policies.

Financial Reporting: Payroll data drives financial planning, budgeting and cost control. Clear records, well-defined procedures, strong systems and robust payroll software support this.

Performance Tracking: Payroll links pay to performance. Good record-keeping, time-tracking software and wage change records are essential tools.

Strategic Decision-Making: Payroll data provides insights into workforce costs, turnover and productivity, helping drive informed, strategic decisions. Reliable records and expert interpretation are key.

I'll talk further on the tools mentioned above later in this chapter.

Payroll data is integral to both the operational and strategic management of a business, providing a foundation for decisions that affect overall financial health, employee satisfaction and operational efficiency.

The Evolution of Business Processes and Payroll's Impact

Payroll has evolved from a basic admin task to a key strategic function that drives business efficiency. Initially, payroll was manual and labour-intensive, highlighting inefficiencies across the business. The shift to automation not only streamlined payroll but influenced other departments to adopt integrated systems, improving overall operations.

Payroll's focus on data accuracy set new standards for consistency across the business, while its role in compliance shaped policies and procedures. The integration of payroll, HR and finance is revolutionising decision-making, providing valuable insights into workforce costs and trends.

The importance put on timely, accurate payroll also improves employee experience, and its approach to data security helps shape broader business protocols. Payroll's continuous innovation, embracing AI (artificial intelligence) and analytics, has driven forward business agility and competitiveness.

Ultimately, payroll has been a driving force for business process evolution, influencing accuracy, compliance, integration and innovation across the board.

What Matters About Processes and Procedures to You and Your Business

Processes and procedures provide a clear path for how work is done, ensuring efficiency, adaptability and growth.

Below, I mention key priorities for you, and how payroll processes and tools can support them.

- **Automation, Technology and Integration:** Automating tasks and integrating systems reduces errors, saves time and boosts efficiency. Payroll leads the way in this, with systems that seamlessly handle calculations, tax deductions and payments. Its success has driven businesses to adopt similar processes across departments, improving collaboration and performance.

- **Continuous Improvement:** Clear, documented processes allow businesses to measure and improve their operations. Payroll's structured, data-driven approach offers insights into workforce management and compliance, setting the tone for continuous refinement throughout the business.

- **Accuracy:** Correct, timely payments keep employees happy and ensure compliance. Payroll's precision influences decision-making, compliance and trust across the business.

- **Record-keeping:** Payroll systems ensure accurate records for audits, financial reporting and compliance. These systems simplify audits and verify expenses, reducing errors and boosting transparency. They also provide a valuable data resource for improving decision-making.

- **Quality and Consistency:** Standardised processes ensure tasks are completed consistently, maintaining quality across the business. Payroll's demand for precision encourages standardisation throughout the business, ensuring reliability and trust.

- **Compliance and Risk Management:** Clear procedures, and checks and controls, help manage risks and maintain compliance with laws and regulations. Payroll is vital in meeting statutory obligations and shaping policies that ensure the business adheres to legal standards.

- **Integration with HR and Finance:** Integrating payroll with HR and finance allows for seamless data sharing, improving strategic decisions on staffing, costs and financial forecasting. Accurate record-keeping aligns departments and enhances efficiency across the business.

- **Efficiency and Productivity:** Streamlined processes help teams work smarter, not harder. Payroll's automated systems handle complex tasks quickly and accurately, freeing time for more strategic work and improving productivity across the board.

- **Flexibility and Agility:** In a fast-moving market, agility is key. Payroll systems are built to adapt to changes in workforce structures, regulations and market trends, helping businesses stay responsive and competitive.

- **Scalability:** As your business grows, payroll systems scale effortlessly, handling complex pay structures and larger teams without losing accuracy or efficiency.

- **Sustainability:** Modern payroll systems reduce paper use and support eco-friendly practices, such as digitising payslips and automating payments, cutting the environmental impact of traditional processes.

- **Client Satisfaction:** Consistent processes lead to great service. Payroll ensures employees are paid on time and accurately, boosting morale and enabling better service for clients.

- **Training and Onboarding:** Payroll supports efficient onboarding through automation, streamlining processes like paperwork, benefits and direct deposits, helping new employees integrate smoothly.

- **Employee Engagement and Well-being:** Accurate, timely payroll builds trust, reduces stress and improves engagement. Clear, reliable workflows and benefits administration contribute to employee satisfaction.

- **Accountability and Performance:** Transparent payroll processes link performance to compensation, motivating employees and creating a culture of accountability.

- **Resource Management:** By automating payments and tracking workforce costs, payroll helps optimise resource use, cutting waste and improving decision-making.

- **Cost Control:** Efficient payroll processes cut costs by reducing errors, optimising staffing and ensuring compliance, ultimately driving profitability and growth.

- **Data-driven Decision-making:** Payroll provides real-time data on salaries, benefits and taxes, helping businesses make informed decisions about budgeting, forecasting and performance.

Payroll is more than just paying employees; it drives efficiency, accuracy and strategic growth across your business. Through this, you can achieve a stronger, more resilient business.

Payroll as a Strategic Tool

In essence, you're looking for processes that drive growth, efficiency and quality, while managing costs, risks and compliance, all with an eye towards sustainability and employee, and ultimately, client satisfaction. Payroll delivers on all of this.

With strong communication and collaboration, in particular with HR and Finance departments, the strategic value of payroll can truly be recognised and utilised.

Below are some of the strengths of payroll that can support your business.

Compliance and Legislation

- **Accuracy and Timeliness:** Payroll systems are designed to ensure that calculations related to taxes, benefits and deductions are accurate and compliant with current laws. Automated updates to tax tables and legal requirements help maintain compliance.
- **Adherence to Employment Laws:** Payroll ensures adherence to employment laws, including minimum wage, overtime and paid leave requirements, thereby avoiding legal disputes and penalties.
- **Audit Readiness:** Proper record-keeping and documentation ensure that payroll is always audit-ready, reducing the risk of non-compliance during audits and further investigations.
- **Data Security:** Payroll systems are built to protect sensitive data, complying with data protection regulations (GDPR).

Processes and Procedures

- **Standardisation:** Well-defined processes and procedures lead to consistency in payroll operations, reducing errors and improving efficiency.
- **Automation:** Automated processes, such as tax calculations, importing of pay data and report generation, minimise manual intervention, which reduces errors and processing time.
- **Scalability:** Standardised procedures make it easier to scale payroll operations as the business grows, ensuring

that payroll can handle increased complexity without compromising accuracy.

- **Continuous Improvement:** Regular reviews and updates to payroll procedures ensure they remain aligned with best practice and evolving business needs.

Structure and Control

- **Segregation of Duties:** Payroll systems and processes are structured to segregate duties (for example, processing, reviewing and authorising), reducing the risk of fraud and errors.
- **Internal Controls:** Strong internal controls, such as approval workflows, access controls and reconciliations help ensure payroll is processed accurately and securely.
- **Compliance with Business Policies:** Payroll's structure supports adherence to business policies regarding compensation, bonuses and other benefits, ensuring fairness and consistency.
- **Risk Management:** Regular audits and control checks help identify potential risks in payroll operations, allowing for proactive mitigation strategies.

Communication

- **Clear Reporting:** Payroll communicates essential financial information to stakeholders, including employees, management and government agencies, in a clear and timely manner.
- **Employee Relations:** Effective communication channels ensure that employees understand their pay, benefits and deductions, reducing confusion and enhancing trust.

- **Feedback Mechanisms:** Payroll often provide avenues for feedback, enabling continuous improvement and quick resolution of any payroll-related issues.
- **Cross-departmental Coordination:** Payroll works closely with HR, Finance and other departments to ensure all relevant information is shared and reflected accurately.

These strengths are critical for maintaining the integrity, efficiency and reliability of payroll operations, thereby supporting the overall stability and reputation of the business. Furthermore, these strengths provide skills that can be transferrable across the business to further your business' operational success.

Payroll teams use a variety of tools to keep processes running smoothly and efficiently, while also providing valuable data for business decisions.

Here's an overview of some of the key tools that support payroll:

CPR for Payroll is a formula I use that ensures all tasks are completed, all data is processed, and accuracy is maintained. This approach is critical for the continued success of payroll operations and keeping your payroll *alive*.

- **C is for Checklist:** Payroll involves juggling many tasks, so checklists are essential. They ensure every step is completed in the right order, minimising the chance of errors and keeping the process consistent and efficient.

- **P is for Pocket:** This is something I picked up from a couple of payroll bureaux I worked in. In the past, we used physical poly pockets in lever arch files to store pending payroll documents. We'd print anything that came in for a client on email, and store anything received in the post in the poly pocket. Now, everything is digital, but the principle remains the same, keeping all relevant information for each payroll in one place to stay organised and ensure nothing is missed. This method can be adapted and works just as well for in-house payroll management, as it does for bureaux.

- **R is for Reconcile:** Payroll data moves through various systems and spreadsheets, and reconciling this data is crucial for accuracy. We compare input sheets with reports from the payroll software to ensure everything matches, making it easy to resolve errors, handle queries and provide transparency during audits. By keeping your process organised and documented, reconciliation ensures that payroll is handled with precision and efficiency.

A **Payroll Calendar** highlights key deadlines at a glance, while the more detailed **Payroll Timeline** breaks down the process step by step. It also shows how payroll interacts with other departments, ensuring a well-structured, consistent approach that keeps everything in sync.

To stay on top of tasks, **Workflow Management Tools** help organise duties and set reminders for important deadlines. These, combined with **Payroll Software**, which automates calculations and data entry, drastically reduce manual errors and keep everything on track, from tracking hours to distributing payslips, all while staying compliant with legal requirements.

Time and Attendance Systems handle the nitty-gritty of tracking working hours, absences and leave, while **ePayslips** offer a quick, efficient and cost-effective way to deliver payslips electronically.

Standardised **Processes and Procedures** ensure consistency and clarity, while **Document Management Systems** securely store payroll-related documents, making them easily accessible for audits or employee queries.

Employee Self-service Portals empower staff to view payslips, update personal information and manage their own benefits, reducing the administrative burden on the payroll team. Collaboration is also enhanced through **Cloud-based Tools**, which allow seamless communication and document sharing across departments, which is especially useful for remote work setups.

Finally, safeguarding sensitive data is crucial. **Data Security Tools** protect payroll information from unauthorised access, ensuring confidentiality and data integrity.

These tools not only streamline payroll operations but also improve accuracy, ensure compliance and provide valuable insights that can inform broader business strategies.

Examples of How Payroll Supports Business Processes

Let's now look at some examples of how payroll can make a difference, to illustrate some of my points.

Compliance and Payroll in a Multi-location Business:

Challenge: A manufacturing business faced compliance challenges due to NMW issues with recording all time worked by employees across its multiple locations. Mismanagement of these regulations resulted in fines, missed deadlines and a growing administrative burden on the payroll team.
Solution: The business provided training to its team on NMW regulations and what was classed as working time. Procedures were documented, distributed and implemented.
Outcome: The business achieved full compliance across its operations, reducing its risk of legal issues and fines. Payroll processing time

was reduced and the business avoided a significant fine that had been imposed previously for non-compliance. The solution enabled the payroll team to focus on strategic functions, while managers and employees gained more trust in the accuracy of their pay.

Reducing Payroll Errors to Improve Employee Satisfaction:

Challenge: A retail chain experienced frequent payroll errors due to the manual entry of employee hours and overtime across multiple locations. This led to a high volume of payroll disputes, employee dissatisfaction and time-consuming corrections.
Solution: The business implemented an automated payroll system, integrated with time and attendance software. This system automatically captured employee work hours and overtime, which was easily transferrable to payroll.
Outcome: The business saw a reduction in payroll disputes soon after implementation. Employee satisfaction improved. HR and payroll teams were able to focus on strategic tasks rather than resolving errors, improving overall efficiency.

Streamlining Onboarding and Payroll Procedures:

Challenge: A construction business, which regularly recruited new employees for specific projects, experienced frequent delays with onboarding new hires into its payroll system, often resulting in late first payslips. This led to poor first impressions and frustration among new employees, impacting retention during the critical first few months of employment.
Solution: The business reviewed and improved the processes and procedures for the flow of information, and the communication channels, between managers, HR and payroll, which allowed for seamless data transfer of onboarding documents and information to payroll. These processes and procedures were documented and distributed to those involved. New employees had clear guidance on

what details they were required to provide, and managers made sure this information was collected as soon as the employee started, and that it was provided to HR and payroll in the required format.

Outcome: Documentation of procedures and clear flow of information meant that everyone involved knew what they needed to do and when. Both HR and payroll reported significantly less manual work, allowing them to focus on employee engagement and support during the onboarding process. New employees had a good onboarding experience, and their expectations were met for the delivery of their pay.

Payroll for Workforce Flexibility and Scheduling Management:

Challenge: A small hospitality group dealt with frequent scheduling changes, which led to errors in calculating pay for employees working irregular hours and overtime. Employees regularly complained about discrepancies in their pay, especially when covering shifts outside of their normal schedule.

Solution: The business implemented an integrated payroll and workforce scheduling system. This system automatically synced employee schedules with payroll, adjusting for overtime, shift differentials and part-time or temporary status changes in real time. Employees were also given access to a self-service portal to verify their work hours and shifts.

Outcome: Payroll discrepancies dropped and employee complaints regarding pay were nearly eliminated. The self-service portal increased transparency, allowing employees to trust that their extra hours or shift changes would be reflected in their pay. Additionally, the business improved its ability to manage workforce costs by gaining real-time insights into staffing expenses.

These examples illustrate how businesses across various industries use payroll data derived from payroll processes and procedures to make strategic decisions, optimise their workforce and, ultimately, improve their business outcomes. You could do the same!

Processes and Procedures, Payroll and You

A well-structured payroll process increases operational efficiency. It reduces the time and effort required to process the payroll, allowing payroll personnel to focus on more strategic tasks - the tasks that can really bring value to your business through enhancing employee experience and maximising efficiencies and productivity. Also, providing you and your management team with the information needed to make informed business decisions that are backed up by relevant data to support easier and more efficient decision-making.

Payroll is one of those professions where change is normal - and expected. We have developed an aptitude for dealing with change and our skills in this area can benefit not just your payroll but your whole business.

'Work smarter, not harder' is a phrase we often hear. It's time to put this into action for yourself and your business. Your health matters and your time is valuable, so don't waste it. Being in business can be very time-draining and stress-inducing, but it doesn't need to be that way. It shouldn't be that way! Make sure your processes and procedures do the hard work and they work for you. Payroll has a big part to play in this. If you can realise the strategic asset that payroll is, then your business will be stronger for it.

Those in the payroll profession continuously learn from each other, to improve the service provided to employees and business owners. It's through this collaboration that our industry grows stronger, more efficient and more valuable for you.

Main Points

- Payroll has evolved from basic data processing to analysing employee behaviour, optimising costs and forecasting financial outcomes. It now plays a strategic role in financial management, compliance, problem-solving and boosting employee engagement. This shift from transactional to transformational highlights payroll's growing impact as a driver of business success.

- Processes and procedures are the backbone of effective business operations. They provide the roadmap for how work is done, ensuring that businesses run smoothly, adapt to change and continue to grow. Well-defined, streamlined processes are essential for maximising productivity while minimising waste and effort.

- By automating repetitive tasks and offering real-time data insights, payroll systems help manage increased operational complexity without adding administrative burden.

- Payroll is more than just paying employees. It drives efficiency, accuracy and strategic growth through strong processes and procedures.

- Payroll data, derived from payroll processes and procedures, helps to make strategic decisions, optimise your workforce and, ultimately, improve your business outcomes. Through detailed analysis of payroll metrics, businesses can gain a clearer picture of how workforce costs impact overall profitability, and adjust strategies accordingly.

Action Points

- **Checklist:** Create a payroll checklist, listing all tasks in the order they need to be done.
- **Payroll Calendar:** Set up a payroll calendar, highlighting key dates and deadlines.
- **Payroll Timeline:** Develop a detailed timeline outlining each task, who's responsible and when, and how information needs to be submitted.
- There are templates available at www.thepayrollguide.co.uk.

People

As businesses evolve, so too does the role of payroll. It is no longer just a back-office function; it has transformed into a crucial component of the employee experience. It's more than just ensuring employees are paid accurately and on time; it's about enhancing their overall experience, satisfaction and retention. A well-functioning payroll system directly impacts whether employees feel valued and engaged, and, in turn, this affects their productivity and loyalty to your business.

An effective payroll function lays the groundwork for a positive employee experience. When employees are confident in their pay and benefits, they are more likely to focus on their roles and contribute to your business' success. This reliability creates trust, reduces anxiety around financial issues and promotes a sense of security.

In this section, I will explore how payroll plays a pivotal role in people management, moving from a mere transactional operation to an experience provider.

I'll start with departments, as they lay the foundations of how a business is structured. Payroll does not exist in isolation; it interacts with various departments, each of which plays a role in shaping the employee experience. By understanding these interactions, we can see how payroll supports the business at a fundamental level.

I'll then shift my focus to employees - the heart of any business. Employee experience is paramount. Satisfied employees are more engaged and less likely to leave. Payroll contributes to this by ensuring that employees feel valued and recognised. When payroll processes are efficient and transparent, employees are empowered to understand their earnings, benefits and deductions clearly. This transparency creates trust and enhances their overall experience.

Next, I'll delve into the interactions between marketing and sales, and payroll. At first glance, these functions might seem disconnected, but they are intricately linked. The way payroll is managed can significantly influence a business' image. A business known for fair pay practices and timely payments will attract and retain talent, thereby enhancing its brand reputation. In a world where employee experience is often a selling point, marketing and sales departments can leverage positive payroll stories in their campaigns, showcasing the business as a desirable place to work.

Finally, I'll discuss reputation, and connect the impacts of payroll on your business' image and brand. In today's digital age, a business' reputation can be built or broken in an instant. Employees who are unhappy with their payroll experience are more likely to voice their concerns publicly, which can tarnish a business' image. Conversely, businesses that prioritise payroll accuracy and transparency build a solid reputation as fair employers. This not only helps in attracting top talent but also enhances client loyalty, as clients increasingly prefer to engage with businesses that treat their employees well.

Payroll is a vital component of people management. By transitioning from a back-office function to an employee experience provider, payroll enhances satisfaction and retention, supporting the overall success of your business. As I explore these topics further, I'll uncover how a robust payroll process can transform not just the Payroll department, but the entire business culture, paving the way for sustainable growth and success.

CHAPTER 7

Departments

Payroll's rhythm guides,
Every department thrives strong,
Unified through trust.

There are many dangers out there for businesses, and the business landscape can be volatile. Over the years we've faced unexpected disasters like Covid-19 and Brexit, which has changed the way we trade with other countries. But it doesn't need to be a nationwide issue to topple a business; it could simply be taking your eye off your local market and competitors, or developing a bad reputation within your local community.

To safeguard against these risks, you must consistently work towards strengthening your business. This means being alert to both the obvious challenges and the less apparent ones. A crucial element in achieving this is ensuring that all departments within your business collaborate towards achieving your common objectives.

Think of a business as a tree. For a tree to grow strong and tall, each part must work well individually and in harmony. The roots need to dig deep to access water and nutrients; the trunk must be tall and sturdy to support strong branches and leaves; and the leaves must absorb sunlight to fuel growth. If any part of the tree fails to function properly, the tree won't flourish. In the same way, a business will struggle to thrive if its departments and people don't perform their roles effectively and work together towards shared goals.

In this chapter, I'll explore some of the main departments within a business, looking at the internal structure and how payroll interacts with each one. I'll talk about the two-way influence between payroll and these departments, and the broader impact this has on the business.

HR (Human Resources)

HR is the natural place to begin, as payroll and HR interact on a daily basis. Each function is heavily reliant on the other to fulfil their responsibilities and ensure compliance with employment regulations.

HR provides payroll with the essential data needed for smooth and efficient processing, from new starter information and contract details, to updates for compensation packages, benefits schemes and changes to the business' structure. Without clear, timely and concise information from HR, payroll cannot function effectively, leading to incorrect payments or deductions for employees. Delays or inaccuracies can put payroll under immense time pressure, and with payroll deadlines being inflexible, this can result in non-compliance, penalties or employees being paid incorrectly, or late.

Mistakes in payroll have devastating consequences for employees (the topic of the next chapter) and equally for the employer. Overpayments affect cash flow, and underpayments can cause significant stress to employees; a critical point given the current economic challenges the country is facing. Moreover, errors in pay can damage employer-employee relationships, demotivating staff and increasing staff turnover, which ultimately hinders the business' growth.

Therefore, strong collaboration between HR and payroll is essential. Together, we generate reports on key metrics like employee headcount, turnover rates, employee demographic analysis and benefit usage. This provides management with the data they need to make informed decisions for the business' future.

Finance

Among other tasks, the Finance department is responsible for ensuring funds are available to pay employees, HMRC, pension providers and other third parties. Without this, payroll cannot function smoothly, which could lead to disgruntled employees and compliance issues due to late payments.

Payroll is also integral to finance reporting, particularly in terms of analysing operational costs. Since wages are typically one of the largest expenses in business, payroll data is crucial for assessing financial stability, planning investments and understanding the business' cash flow. Payroll provides the financial numbers that underpin these reports, including journals detailing payroll costs and amounts due to external parties, ensuring accurate accounting of the 'human cost' of your business.

Payroll also supports the Finance department in forecasting and budgeting, especially when it comes to the costs associated with expanding the workforce or implementing pay rises.

Depending on the size and structure of your business, there are regulation requirements for certain data to be recorded, retained and reported to various bodies. Payroll helps ensure compliance within the business' financial reporting requirements, and assists management in making all-important decisions.

Marketing and Sales

Although two distinct roles within a business, I've grouped marketing and sales together as they have the same main purpose - to bring revenue into the business. I won't talk much on these here as I'll go into the impact and interactions payroll can have with marketing and sales, later, in Chapter 9.

For now, note that sales teams are often incentivised through commission-based pay structures, meaning their earnings are directly linked to performance. If communication breaks down regarding the calculation of commissions, or if payroll errors occur, it undermines the motivational purpose to their pay structure, and can lead to frustration and demotivation within the sales team. It's crucial that marketing, sales and payroll maintain strong lines of communication to prevent these issues.

Additionally, marketing relies heavily on the reputation and image of a business, something which payroll has a strong influence on.

IT (Information Technology)

As payroll increasingly relies on technology, the support of the IT department is essential. From storing sensitive data securely, to maintaining reliable payroll systems, IT plays a key role in ensuring payroll runs smoothly. The Covid-19 pandemic highlighted the importance of having robust systems in place, with remote access to payroll software becoming essential.

There was an incident faced by a well-known employer, Twitter, in November 2022[08]. Business Insider reported on its website that Twitter's Payroll department, and a large portion of its Finance department, left the company in a mass resignation due to an ultimatum the new owner, Elon Musk, had made to employees. It's said that around 50% of Twitter's employees took the voluntary redundancy being offered, instead of signing up to Twitter 2.0.

Now, depending on how resource-heavy Twitter was, they might have been able to function for a while with that size of employee loss. However, with the whole Payroll department leaving, how did that affect the functioning of the business? Who was going to pay the

50% of employees who chose to stay? How long would they stay, with disruption and uncertainty around their pay?

Incidents like Twitter's mass employee walkout in 2022 illustrate the importance of having contingency plans. When key departments such as payroll leave, businesses face a huge risk of being unable to pay remaining staff. Business continuity planning, supported by IT, is essential to safeguard against such disruptions.

Operations

Clear and effective communication is crucial for ensuring a smooth flow of information between payroll and the Operations department. This is particularly true when it comes to gathering essential details such as employee working hours, holidays, sick leave and any updates to personal details. Timesheets, or tracking hours worked, are often viewed as a dreaded task by employees and managers alike. However, it is a critical part of the payroll process. Mistakes or delays in submitting timesheets not only lead to incorrect or late payments, but they have the potential to throw the entire payroll process into disarray.

While the operations team is understandably focused on day-to-day tasks, it's important they recognise the vital role that prompt and accurate communication with payroll plays. Any breakdown in this flow of information can significantly increase the workload and stress levels of the payroll team, and, in turn, affect the overall efficiency of the business.

Managers don't want to be bogged down with constant pay-related queries from their teams; they need employees to focus on their work. By establishing and maintaining strong communication channels between operations and payroll, we can ensure any issues are handled swiftly and correctly. This means employees get the answers they need without delay, allowing them to get back to their tasks without unnecessary interruptions, keeping everything running smoothly.

Management

I've deliberately left management until last. Whilst the interaction between other departments is important, it is the management team that determines the strategic direction of the business, the products and services the business is going to make or provide, and the budgets, which in turn impacts payroll.

Whether it's changes in employee numbers, benefits or business structure, payroll needs to be involved in these conversations early to ensure smooth implementation. Early engagement allows payroll to plan ahead, offering valuable insights and ensuring that processes and procedures are adapted to accommodate the change.

Payroll provides management with crucial statistical data that supports decision-making, from cash-flow management to cost projections for pay rises. Strong collaboration between payroll and the management team is vital for the overall success of the business.

Each department within a business relies on payroll in different ways, and the success of the business depends on strong, clear communication and collaboration. By involving payroll early in key decisions, and ensuring timely and accurate data flow, you can avoid costly mistakes and ensure your employees remain motivated and engaged.

For small businesses like mine, the departmental structure has not been developed yet. But each business with aspirations to grow should consider the internal departmental and employee structure required for each stage of growth, so that cash-flow planning is in place to ensure business stability within growth. Always start with the end in mind; it makes it much easier to navigate to where you aspire to be.

You might find yourself wearing multiple hats, essentially running several departments within your business all on your own. Whether you're handling operations, HR, finance, marketing and even a bit of payroll, it's not uncommon in smaller businesses or when you're in the early stages of growth. While this can be a cost-effective way to get things moving, it's also incredibly demanding and can stretch your time and resources. Trying to juggle everything yourself means that certain tasks may end up being rushed, overlooked or done half-heartedly, simply because there aren't enough hours in the day.

It's important to recognise when this approach starts to become unsustainable. As your business grows, so too does the complexity of managing different functions, and what might have worked at the beginning can quickly become a bottleneck to progress. You could be missing opportunities to focus on strategic growth, simply because you're caught up in the day-to-day admin of running the show. Careful consideration to your business' internal structure and employee requirements should be made and regularly reviewed.

In the next chapter, I'll dive into the individual components of your business, your employees, how payroll affects them and, in turn, how their actions impact the payroll process.

Main Points

- Your business is like a tree. For the tree to grow strong and tall, it needs every part of it to function well, and together.
- Strong collaboration is needed between payroll and other departments to ensure the timely and accurate flow of information.
- A good proportion of the reports payroll can assist with are statistical, fact-based reports that tell the business' story in numbers, or personnel-based, reporting on demographics and employee structure. All these reports assist you and your management team to analyse your business and make informed decisions for the future.
- As the years go by, we are seeing an increase in the use and importance of technology and systems in the payroll process. The continuity and reliability of the systems used is highly important in ensuring that employees get paid accurately and on time.
- Involving payroll early in business changes or implementations allows us to use our expertise and strategic insight to support projects and people-based changes, and help achieve your business goals.

Action Points

- **Roles and Responsibilities:** Map the roles and responsibilities for each department in relation to payroll, and payroll's responsibilities to each department. Provide clear and concise expectations for communication, responsibilities, and a better and more timely flow of information.

Chapter Endnotes

8 Kali Hays, Business Insider, Twitter loses Payroll department, other financial employees as part of mass resignation under Elon Musk, 18th November 2022, as viewed 17th February 2025: https://www.businessinsider.com/twitter-payroll-finance-department-resigns-en-masse-under-elon-musk-2022-11?r=US&IR=T

CHAPTER 8

Employees

Timely, fair payroll,
Keeps hearts light and spirits high,
Employees thrive strong.

One of the biggest steps a business can take on its journey, is that of hiring a team, and it's part of the natural evolution for most businesses. There's no point hiding from it. Embrace it and remember that it is through hiring a team that your dreams and the life you want your business to facilitate, will be realised.

While employees are the heart of your business and your number one asset, people have different wants and needs; different motivations and personalities. To get a group of people together, to motivate them into being productive, with the same focus, aligned to the same objectives, a gelled team that can push your business forward is no easy feat.

Your employees' influence is woven into every aspect of your business, from its daily operations to its long-term vision. They drive your business' performance, set the tone for client relationships, fuel innovation and bring the business' values to life. Every task they perform, decision they make and interaction they have leaves a lasting impact.

In this chapter, I'll delve into the critical importance of truly understanding your employees. I'll explore not just what your workforce wants, but also the hurdles they face, equipping you with insight that's vital for effective leadership. From there, I'll address the pivotal role of recruitment and people management, tackling some of the common challenges you'll face. I'll also unpack employee demographics and dive into why having a deep understanding of your team is not only beneficial, but essential for driving success and creating a thriving, engaged workforce.

Whether it's meeting targets, solving problems or representing the business to the outside world, employees are at the heart of everything, shaping the business' success from the ground up. What follows is why they're so crucial.

Productivity: Employees are the ones who turn strategy into action. They handle the day-to-day work, from delivering services to making products, and their dedication directly impacts efficiency and profitability. Without their hard work, even the best business plan wouldn't stand a chance.

Client Experience: Employees are the face of your business. How they interact with clients shapes your business' reputation. Their professionalism, attitude and service can make or break client relationships, driving satisfaction, loyalty and repeat business. A strong team keeps clients coming back.

Innovation: Employees are the engine behind fresh ideas. Their unique perspectives and problem-solving skills fuel the creativity that helps your business adapt, grow and stay ahead of the competition. Encouraging their input can lead to new products or services, improved processes and smart solutions.

Culture and Brand: Employees are key to building a positive work environment. Their buy-in to your business' values strengthens team morale and attracts top talent. As brand ambassadors, they enhance your reputation inside and outside the business, making it a place people want to associate with.

Growth and Revenue: Every employee, whether on the front line or behind the scenes, plays a role in growing the business. Their ability to solve problems, adapt to challenges and work as a team ensures smooth operations and long-term success. They are the driving force behind revenue generation and business expansion.

Employees aren't just part of the business; they *are* the business. Investing in them means investing in your business' future success.

Your People

Understanding and supporting employees is vital to creating a positive and productive workplace. Employees are not only the driving force behind a business' operations, but their well-being, motivation and engagement directly impact its success.

Here's a breakdown of what's most important for creating a strong employer-employee relationship:

Understanding Your Employees

A strong business starts with understanding its people. This includes effective communication, being culturally aware and respecting the work-life balance your employees need. Listening to their concerns and being responsive to their feedback creates trust and loyalty. Embracing diversity and promoting inclusivity are essential for building a supportive work culture. Employees want to feel valued, heard and understood, which can be as simple as considering their needs when making business decisions. You can achieve this even if you're a small business with limited resources.

What Employees Want

To feel engaged and motivated, employees expect fair treatment, opportunities for growth and job security. Clear communication, both in terms of business direction and individual feedback, is crucial. They want competitive and fair pay, benefits and flexibility, particularly in balancing personal and work life, and increasingly seek autonomy to perform their roles without micromanagement. Opportunities for career development, recognition for achievements and a supportive work environment are key factors in retaining top talent. Employees want to feel their work is meaningful, that they're trusted and that you value their contribution to your business' success.

The Challenges Employees Face

Despite the best efforts of businesses, employees often face issues that affect their work satisfaction and performance. One of the most common is payroll problems, whether it's errors in payment, late wages or a lack of transparency about how pay is calculated. This can create frustration and financial strain, damaging trust between employees and employers. Addressing these challenges with accurate, transparent and flexible payroll processes and procedures is crucial to maintain a positive relationship and ensure employees feel secure and respected in their roles. When businesses get these basics right, it goes a long way towards building a happy, productive workforce.

By addressing these core areas, understanding employees, meeting their needs and resolving common challenges, you can create a working environment where employees feel valued, motivated and committed to your business' long-term success.

Recruiting and People Management

With employees being so important for businesses, it makes the recruitment process even more crucial to get right. Employers face a variety of payroll-related challenges when hiring and managing employees, which can impact their ability to build an effective team, and employee satisfaction. These challenges not only influence how businesses attract and retain talent, but also have a direct impact on compliance, financial management and business culture.

The number of job vacancies in the UK for June to August 2024, as estimated by the Office for National Statistics, stood at 857,000[09]. Although job vacancies have declined since Covid-19, and candidate availability has risen, this still presents a highly competitive recruitment market for employers; the extent of which is heavily dependent on the demographics required for the position. Numerous factors are involved in recruitment difficulties, but most can be associated with payroll-related aspects.

Hiring is tough; I know that firsthand. I'm early in my journey as an employer, having started in 2021. By the end of that year, I knew I needed help, so I hired a part-time trainee. This wasn't just about bringing someone into the profession, but about managing finances, cash flow and time. Starting small made sense. Lower costs and more flexibility meant I could test the waters of being an employer without overcommitting. It also allowed me to quickly hire a second person, ensuring cover for holidays and sickness.

My first hire didn't work out, and health issues meant I paused recruiting. By July 2022, I tried again, but once more, it wasn't a good fit. Hiring during Covid-19 added extra challenges, but these false starts taught me more about what I really needed in an employee. It's tough to get everything right – skills, character, work ethic – but that's part of the process. Often, it takes at least six months before you can tell how an employee is going to work out. By October 2022, my third hire finally worked out.

In 2023, I needed to expand. I was looking for someone with more experience, but finding candidates within my budget was difficult. I hired another employee in August 2023, but we quickly realised it wasn't working. So, I returned to hiring a trainee, despite the challenges of training from scratch, which takes extra time and effort. This said, I enjoy introducing the payroll profession to new people.

I work from home, as do my employees, with regular training in my home office. It takes about six months to train someone until they can start supporting and contributing to the business, which is a big investment of time and money, but essential for growth. Remote working has its benefits, though training remotely can be tricky.

In March 2024, I hired another trainee who's been a fast learner and a great asset to the team. I'm incredibly grateful to my team. As the team grows, so do the challenges of managing different personalities, skills and experience, but it's all part of the journey, so take it step by step and you'll learn a lot during the process.

There have been plenty of bumps along the way, but that's normal, especially in today's market. If things don't work out with an employee, it's fine; you're testing the fit for both sides. If it's not working, try something different; not everyone responds to the same training methods. Learn from it, but ultimately if it's not working, then for the sake of both parties, you both need to move on.

Below are some of the challenges you may encounter:

Finding Qualified Talent: One of the biggest challenges is finding candidates with the right skills, experience and cultural fit. Skill shortages in certain industries or roles, particularly in highly specialised fields like technology or healthcare, make recruitment difficult, time-consuming and costly.

High Competition for Talent: In competitive job markets, employers must contend with other businesses offering attractive salaries, benefits and perks. Standing out from the crowd, to attract top talent to your business, often requires more substantial compensation and benefit packages, which can strain budgets.

Complex Salary Negotiations: Employers often face difficulties in offering competitive yet sustainable salaries. Understanding market rates for different roles, including the varying expectations for benefits, bonuses and incentives, can be complex. Over or underestimating salary offers can result in either financial strain for the business or difficulty attracting the right talent.

Compliance with Wage Laws: Employers must adhere to NMW (National Minimum Wage) requirements, overtime and paid leave regulations. During hiring (particularly for diverse roles across multiple locations, including international), varying work patterns (creating complexity and difficulties in recording hours worked) and business structure (ensuring workers' contract types are correctly identified) can lead to legal issues and fines.

Legal and Regulatory Compliance: Employers must navigate an array of employment laws and regulations, including employment standards, NMW, non-discrimination policies, health and safety requirements, and employment law. Missteps in ensuring compliance can result in penalties, legal issues and damage to the business' reputation (I'll be delving into reputation in Chapter 10).

Managing Different Worker Types: Businesses may employ full-time, part-time, salaried or hourly paid employees with varying shift patterns, or contractors and gig workers - each with unique payroll, benefits and legal implications. Correctly classifying workers and managing their compensation are essential to avoid legal and tax issues.

Managing Payroll and Benefits: Establishing fair and compliant payroll processes, offering competitive benefits and handling the administrative aspects of employee compensation are intricate tasks.

Providing benefits, such as pensions, health insurance, company cars and cycle-to-work schemes, can help attract top talent, but managing these benefits through payroll can be challenging, particularly during onboarding. Employers must integrate benefits administration with payroll systems to ensure accurate deductions and compliance. Payroll mistakes can result in employee dissatisfaction and potentially lead to legal complications.

Adapting to Remote Working: With the rise of remote and hybrid work models, employers face challenges in managing a dispersed workforce. This includes maintaining productivity, building team cohesion, setting up remote payroll systems and ensuring compliance with diverse location-specific regulations, like tax rates and threshold for Scottish, Rest of the UK and Welsh resident workers. This complexity deepens even further when employees work internationally.

Onboarding and Integration: Bringing new hires up to speed is crucial to their success and retention. An inadequate onboarding process can leave new employees feeling unsupported, impacting their performance and increasing the likelihood of early turnover.

Onboarding Delays and Payroll Setup: Efficiently setting up new hires in the payroll system is crucial to accurate and timely payments. However, delays in collecting necessary documentation (e.g. names, addresses, National Insurance numbers and starter declaration statements) can result in payment issues, creating a negative first impression for new employees.

Handling Payroll for Variable Compensation: For roles that involve commission, bonuses or overtime, accurately calculating and including these variable components in payroll can be challenging. Employers must track and process this information promptly and accurately to ensure employees are compensated correctly, which adds complexity to payroll management.

Balancing Costs, Budgeting and Forecasting: I'll go over payroll costs more in the Profit section, but for now, hiring employees comes with a financial burden beyond just salaries, including benefits, training, insurances and equipment. Employers need to balance these costs, offering competitive compensation, with maintaining a sustainable payroll budget, along with the benefits of expanding their workforce. Poor payroll forecasting can lead to cash-flow issues, especially for small businesses, making it difficult to expand the workforce or provide timely raises and bonuses.

Tax Withholding and Reporting: Hiring employees requires accurate tax withholding based on their residency status, work location and pay structure. Mistakes in setting up new employees on the wrong tax table can lead to incorrect pay and compliance risks, requiring adjustments that complicate payroll processing and confuse employees.

Navigating Payroll Systems: Employers, especially small businesses, may lack the infrastructure for a robust payroll system. This is where outsourcing the payroll often helps. As the workforce grows, manually handling payroll can become error-prone and time-consuming, increasing the likelihood of mistakes in pay and benefits.

Offering Flexible Pay Options: Many employees are now looking for more flexible pay options or more often pay frequencies, which has led to the introduction of on-demand pay. While these options can be attractive during hiring, they require payroll systems capable of handling such flexibility, adding complexity to payroll administration, and they come with big responsibilities for employers. Within the UK over the last 10–15 years, there has been a marked decrease in the number of weekly payrolls, with employers favouring a monthly pay frequency in order to reduce processing time and costs. This requires a level of budgeting and forward planning on the employees' part, to manage their finances.

Retaining Employees: Retention is a major concern for employers, especially when skilled employees leave for better opportunities. High turnover can disrupt productivity, increase costs and negatively impact team morale.

Handling Diversity and Inclusion: Building a diverse workforce is crucial but can be challenging. Employers need to create an inclusive environment where all employees feel valued, which requires ongoing effort in training, policy-making and addressing unconscious biases (social stereotypes about certain groups of people that individuals form outside their own conscious awareness[10]).

Training and Development: Once employees are hired, employers need to invest in training and professional development to ensure they have the skills necessary for their roles. This requires time, resources and a strategic approach to employee growth.

Performance Management: Effectively assessing and managing employee performance can be difficult. Employers must establish clear expectations, provide regular feedback and address performance issues constructively, all while maintaining motivation and engagement.

Mental Health and Well-being: Employers are increasingly responsible for supporting employee well-being, particularly amid workplace stress and changing work environments. Providing support systems and balancing productivity with well-being concerns requires careful management.

Cultural Fit and Integration: Employers need to find candidates who not only have the required skills but fit well within the business' culture and team dynamics. Mismatches can lead to friction within teams and a decrease in overall morale and productivity.

These difficulties require you to take a strategic, flexible approach to hiring, training and managing your workforce, to build a productive and engaged team, while minimising potential risks and challenges.

For example, an employer I worked with had built a team of nine, gearing up for a product launch when Covid-19 hit. He'd been paying them well, offering higher pension contributions than required. His intentions were good, and I commend him for that. However, with the product still in development, he relied on bank funding, which dried up during the pandemic. Sadly, he had to let his entire team go.

The lack of funding would have halted the business regardless, but had he been more cautious with the generous pension contributions and salaries, could the business have lasted longer? Maybe long enough for funding to resume? We'll never know. My point is, while we all want to be great employers and offer the benefits we wish we had when we were working as an employee, we must ensure the business can sustain it. You can always increase pay and perks later, when cash flow is stable, but cutting back is much harder.

When expanding your team, it's key to be clear on the exact skills and personal traits you need. For me, soft skills are far more important than technical experience. You can teach the job, but you can't teach good work ethic, reliability or a positive attitude.

Employee Demographics

Employee demographics refer to the various characteristics that define your workforce, such as age, gender, ethnicity, education level, job roles, years of service, and many more. These details provide valuable insights that can inform recruitment, workforce planning and business strategy. Understanding these demographic factors allow businesses to make informed decisions that directly influence growth, diversity and overall performance.

This data is important for the following reasons:

Informed Recruitment

By analysing employee demographics, you can spot gaps in your current workforce, whether in skills, experience or gender pay balance. This insight helps shape targeted recruitment strategies. Just as businesses create a 'client avatar' to guide marketing efforts, an 'employee avatar' can be created to define the ideal candidate for specific roles, helping you attract the right talent more efficiently. This approach streamlines hiring, reduces the likelihood of recruitment mistakes and ensures you're building a balanced, capable team.

Succession Planning

Demographic data, especially age and tenure, is crucial for planning future staffing needs. It highlights which employees may be approaching retirement or other career changes. By identifying these trends early, you can prepare for knowledge transfer, ensuring key roles remain filled without disruptions to the business. It allows for a smoother transition by equipping successors with the necessary skills and understanding well in advance.

Boosting Diversity and Inclusion

Employee demographics are key to assessing how diverse and inclusive your workplace is. They help you track representation across different groups, allowing you to implement initiatives that create an inclusive culture. A diverse workforce enhances creativity, problem-solving and innovation by bringing together different perspectives and experiences. Promoting inclusivity not only boosts employee morale and retention, but also strengthens your business' reputation, making it more attractive to top talent.

Tailoring Benefits

Different demographic groups often have varying needs and preferences when it comes to benefits and perks. Younger employees may prioritise development opportunities, while those with families might seek flexible working or better parental leave options. By understanding these needs, you can tailor your benefits package to meet the diverse expectations of your workforce, improving satisfaction and retention across the board.

Driving Innovation and Engagement

A diverse team, informed by demographic insights, naturally brings a wider range of ideas and experiences. This diversity fuels innovation, leading to creative solutions and helping the business adapt to challenges. In addition, analysing demographics can reveal trends in employee engagement and turnover, allowing you to pinpoint which groups might be less satisfied. From there, you can create targeted strategies to improve their experience, driving higher engagement and retention.

Demographics like age, gender and ethnicity need particular care in terms of what data is collected, stored and how it's used, to ensure compliance with employment laws like those

I mentioned in Chapter 2, and to ensure you're operating ethically. There are many advantages to having a diverse demographic in your business. Demographic analysis in payroll is not for the purpose of discrimination and should never be used in that way. It is for the purpose of understanding your numbers and how changes to your business might affect them. Demographics serve as a valuable tool for shaping business strategy, culture and practices. Understanding and utilising employee demographics allows businesses to recruit smarter, plan more effectively and build a diverse, innovative workforce. This data, when used thoughtfully, leads to better decision-making, higher employee satisfaction and stronger business outcomes.

Benefits of Understanding Your Employees

Understanding what your employees want from their employment and payroll is crucial for any business, directly influencing productivity, retention and overall performance.

Here's why it matters:

Boosting Retention: When employees feel valued, job satisfaction increases, and they're more likely to stay. This reduces the costs of constant hiring, onboarding and training. Businesses that listen to their teams create stronger, longer-lasting relationships with their workforce.

Increasing Productivity and Engagement: A valued employee is a motivated one. By catering to needs like flexible working, pay structures and benefits, you create a positive environment where people are engaged and driven to perform. This translates into higher productivity, as engaged staff are more likely to go the extra mile and work proactively.

Attracting Top Talent: Today's workforce need their pay, but they're looking for more than just a payslip. Flexible working, development opportunities and a strong work-life balance matter. Tailoring your benefits package to reflect these priorities will help you stand out in the job market, making it easier to attract the best talent and improve your employer brand.

Customising Compensation and Benefits: Understanding what your employees truly value allows you to optimise your benefits offering, cutting costs on underused perks and focusing on what matters most. Flexible working options or performance bonuses can enhance your overall package, increasing its appeal without unnecessary expense.

Supporting Well-being: Addressing payroll concerns and offering financial wellness support, alongside flexible working, reduces employee stress. A healthy, less-stressed workforce is not only more productive but more engaged, and employees who feel supported are more likely to thrive long term.

Enhancing Adaptability: Different employees have different priorities. Some value flexibility, others prioritise retirement plans or career growth. Recognising these differences allows you to adapt to workforce demands, keeping your business competitive in a rapidly changing job market.

Understanding and acting on employee needs leads to a more loyal, engaged and productive workforce. This strategic approach not only benefits your employees but enhances your overall business performance and competitive advantage.

Main Points

- Employees are a business' most valuable asset. They're not just resources, but the pulse of the business. Their skills, motivation, engagement and alignment with the business' goals are critical to driving success, innovation and sustainable growth.

- You need to take a strategic, flexible approach to hiring, training and managing your workforce to build a productive and engaged team, while minimising potential risks and challenges.

- Employees need several key elements from their employers to feel valued, motivated and productive. These needs can significantly influence job satisfaction, performance and overall retention.

- Inaccuracies in payments, delays, lack of clarity around deductions, poor communication or discrepancies in overtime and bonuses can lead to an unsatisfied employee. Such payroll issues can erode trust between employees and employer, impacting morale and, ultimately, performance.

- Employee demographics serve as a valuable tool for shaping a business' strategy, culture and practices. When used thoughtfully and sensitively, this data enables you to create a more inclusive, adaptable and effective workforce, with a dynamic set of skills and experiences, ultimately driving better business outcomes.

Action Points

- **Employee Avatar:** When hiring, create an employee avatar based on demographics to define your ideal candidate. This helps clarify what you need, making recruitment easier.

- **Employee Analysis:** Review your current staff structure, roles, skills and other demographics to understand your position. Identify gaps and unmet needs to ensure business success.

Chapter Endnotes

9 Office for National Statistics, Census 2021, Vacancies and jobs in the UK: September 2024, released 10th September 2024, as viewed 17th February 2025: https://www.ons.gov.uk/employmentandlabourmarket/peopleinwork/employmentandemployeetypes/bulletins/jobsandvacanciesintheuk/september2024#:~:text=The%20estimated%20number%20of%20vacancies,in%20all%2018%20industry%20sectors

10 J. Renee Navarro, PharmD, MD, UCSF Office of Diversity and Outreach, as viewed 17th February 2025: https://diversity.ucsf.edu/programs-resources/training/unconscious-bias-training#:~:text=Unconscious%20biases%20are%20social%20stereotypes,organize%20social%20worlds%20by%20categorizing

CHAPTER 9

Marketing and Sales

Payroll steady, fair,
Happy teams drive sales with pride,
Marketing blooms wide.

When deciding where to spend our money, whether as consumers or in B2B (business-to-business) relationships, we often gravitate towards businesses that demonstrate social responsibility. We hold these businesses in higher regard than those that don't.

We see the businesses we support as extensions of our own values.

Choosing a socially responsible business allows us to contribute to society or the environment, without much effort on our part, making us feel good in the process. That's why it's crucial for your business to reflect your beliefs and values. This not only draws in clients but, more importantly, the right kind of clients.

People buy from people. It's a simple truth. How your team represents your business and embodies its values are crucial to creating the right impression. Have you ever walked into a shop, asked a question, and been met with a rude or unhelpful response? Or overheard staff grumbling about their pay? We've all been there, and it doesn't inspire confidence. It's often enough to make you take your money elsewhere, no matter how much you like the products or service that business provides.

When choosing to buy a product or service, it's not just about price; it's about what the business stands for and whether its values align with your own. Take the iPhone, for example. It's not drastically different from other handsets, but its brand and vision make it stand out. As Simon Sinek said in his book, *Start with Why*, "People don't buy what you do; they buy why you do it."[11]

All the adverts and PR in the world won't achieve lasting success if your team doesn't live and breathe the values you want to be known for.

In this chapter, I'll delve into the vital link between your employees and the success of your marketing and sales efforts, highlighting how their performance directly influences your business' growth. A well-supported, motivated and skilled team is crucial to driving effective marketing strategies and generating sales, ensuring your customers are engaged and loyal. I'll explore how issues like poor compensation, ineffective communication, or lack of role clarity can lead to disengaged employees, which negatively affects your marketing outcomes and customer interactions. Additionally, I'll look at the importance of recruitment, talent management and maintaining accurate payroll processes. A strong foundation in employee management not only enhances your marketing and sales outcomes but also creates sustainable growth and long-term success.

How your staff interact with clients has a direct impact on whether they'll choose to do business with you, and how much business they'll bring your way. That's why, as a business leader, it's your responsibility to ensure your team is happy, well-trained and productive, so it can deliver the best possible service to your clients. If employees are disgruntled due to payroll issues or confusion over their hours, they'll struggle to provide that all-important five-star service. The human element, therefore, plays a key role in the strength, direction and growth of your business.

Valuing your employees and getting payroll (the cornerstone of the employer-employee relationship) right, should be your top priority. If you get this wrong, the foundations of your business may not hold, and everything could crumble when you least expect it.

Know, Like and Trust

Do you enjoy networking? Personally, it doesn't come naturally to me. As an introvert, I have to make a real effort to push myself. Referral networking is a brilliant way to generate business, but it takes time, effort and practice to get right. In many small businesses, it's often the owner doing the networking, but that's not always the case. If you've got an employee representing your business, it's crucial they're in the right headspace, happy with their job, pay and working conditions, so they can leave a positive and lasting impression.

The last thing you want is for the conversation to shift towards frustrations like unpaid commissions or other grievances. These concerns often linger in an employee's mind, and I've lost count of the number of times I've been at a networking event, chatting with a sales rep, only for them to start venting about their pay as soon as they realise I work in payroll. It's a situation that can quickly harm your business' reputation, so it's definitely something to be mindful of.

The concept of 'know, like and trust' has long been a cornerstone of marketing – coined by Bob Burg in his book, *Endless Referrals*[12]. He explains: "All things being equal, people will do business with, and refer business to, those they know, like and trust." We all get the importance of this, but how does payroll fit into the picture?

Know

Your clients need to know you, not personally, but they need to have a clear sense of who you are as a business and what you stand for. There's no easier way to attract new business than through word-of-mouth referrals. When someone who knows your business speaks highly of you and refers a potential client, that person is more likely to trust that you'll deliver on your promises, making them easier to convert into a client.

Spending money with a business you don't know carries a high level of risk and uncertainty, which can lead to stress and hesitation. While referrals from contacts help establish trust, so does your consistent presence on social media, where you're transparent and provide value to your audience.

But it's not just you that potential clients will come to know. When they enquire about your products or services, or make a purchase, they'll primarily interact with your employees. If your team provides a poor first impression or bad service, it leaves a lasting negative impact. Unfortunately, people tend to remember negative experiences more vividly than positive ones. So, it's essential that your employees not only represent your brand but also embody its values to build that all-important trust.

Like

It's one thing for clients to know your business, but they also need to like what they know about you, your business and your team, before they'll want to work with you.

In the past, business owners and CEOs often stayed behind the scenes, driving the vision and ensuring goals were met. But today, more business leaders are stepping into the public eye. As consumers, we no longer want faceless brands; we want to know the person behind the business and what they stand for. Take Richard Branson, for example. He's the face of the Virgin Group, known for his people-centric approach across all his ventures. Like Branson, I'm the face of my business. Although clients might interact with a team member, it's my values, experience and knowledge that attract clients to work with us. And the same goes for you. You are the face of your business, and it's your values and beliefs that can draw people in and convince them you're the right choice for their business.

But it's not just about who leads the business. For clients to truly like your business, they also need to like your team, since they're the ones your clients will be dealing with day-to-day. Your team's values and focus need to align with yours, reflecting what you want your business to stand for. That said, this isn't their business; they're working for you to get paid. If you let them down on something as vital as their pay, what motivation will they have to uphold your values when dealing with your clients? You can train your staff thoroughly, giving them the knowledge and skills to deliver five-star service, but if they're distracted by worries about their pay, it's all too easy for standards to slip.

Trust

Lastly, your clients need to trust you and your team.

Trust can often come down to a gut feeling, or it might stem from hearing about unethical practices in the news, like when a business mistreats its employees, which can make us hesitate to buy from them as we lose trust in that business.

It is like with the 'name and shame' list that HMRC publishes, containing employers who have not met their NMW responsibilities. Some well-known businesses make that list. Would you trust a business once you saw them on this list? If they can't pay their employees fairly and legally, how much confidence would you have in their ability to provide you with a good and fair service? If an employee finds out they've been underpaid, how motivated will they be to deliver great service to your client? And on principle, many of us simply don't want to give our money to businesses that behave unethically and fail to value their staff.

Payroll legislation is complex and constantly changing, and as a small business owner, you have enough on your plate. You didn't go into business to get bogged down in admin and paperwork, but it's something that needs your attention, because the well-being of your staff is fundamental to the success of your business.

For your clients to trust you, you must hold yourself and your business to account. You need to act responsibly and, for most businesses, this begins with how you treat your team.

All the marketing content you put out about your business and all the effort made by your marketing and sales teams are meaningless if the client experience doesn't live up to these promises. Bad experiences undermine your marketing and sales efforts, breeding mistrust around your business. And we all know how damaging bad word of mouth can be. It's what I call the 'breath of death' for a business. Every bad word breathed about your business, whether from a dissatisfied client or an unhappy employee, damages your reputation. As I'll explore further in the following chapter, a tarnished reputation is not easy to recover from.

These principles are essential to running a successful business. Ignore them, and your business will suffer.

Why Payroll Should Be Part of Your Marketing Plan

The key point here is that your employees' attitude towards their work, and how they feel about their treatment and pay, directly affects their interactions with your clients. Your team can have a significant impact on your marketing and sales efforts, so it makes sense to include them in your marketing strategy.

You should consider developing a marketing plan that includes payroll. It might sound odd at first, but if your employees have the biggest influence on how well marketing and sales perform and, ultimately, on whether people buy from your business, why wouldn't you include payroll, the aspect most important to your employees, in your marketing plan?

This part of your marketing plan will largely be for internal use, but its impact will be felt outside the business too. Start by reviewing your payroll processes and procedures (as covered in the Process section) to ensure they're as robust as possible to minimise errors.

Payroll can never be 100% accurate – it's too complex, with too many variables – but strong processes and systems can get it pretty close.

Another key element is communication, covered in Chapter 5. Keeping your employees well-informed about the various aspects of their pay and benefits throughout the payroll process is essential. Employees are far more forgiving of the occasional error if they feel they're kept in the loop and receive clear, honest answers to their questions.

Next, build a Payroll Protocol. A protocol is a set of rules outlining proper conduct and procedures in formal situations. In this case, your Payroll Protocol should detail what employees should do if they discover an error in their pay or have a query, and how payroll should handle these concerns. The protocol should include response times and flag peak payroll processing periods when responses might take longer, thereby managing expectations. This can help reduce confusion, frustration and preserve trust between employer and employee.

Additionally, I'd recommend creating an Employee Client Engagement Protocol – guidelines for how your staff should behave around clients. It might seem obvious, but providing clear instructions and explaining how even a casual grumble about pay can impact the business, and by extension their own job security, can be helpful. If fewer sales come in, there's less money for wages, after all. This protocol should also outline how employees can voice any concerns they have about their pay, without it affecting client relations.

Including payroll in your marketing plan isn't just about preventing negative client experiences; it's an opportunity to boost positivity around your business. Highlighting how well you treat your staff makes for great, engaging social media content and helps build a sense of community around your brand. It attracts talent, making people want to work for you, and it draws clients in, who feel confident buying from a business that values its people.

Don't leave your clients' impression of your business to chance; it's far too important.

Main Points

- We look at the businesses we buy from to be an extension of our own values and beliefs. People buy from people.

- Negative experiences can be more memorable than positive ones. Bad client experiences undermine your marketing and sales efforts, and build mistrust around your business. We all know how far and wide bad experiences can spread by word of mouth.

- Clear processes for handling employee queries and client interactions prevent confusion and ensure consistency.

- Payroll should be included in your marketing plan to help mitigate against negative client experiences and boost positive marketable opportunities.

- How you handle and approach your payroll responsibilities leaves an impression on your clients. Your clients' impression of your business is far too important to be left to chance.

Action Points

- **Payroll Marketing Plan:** Create a marketing plan around your employees and your payroll. Identify the touch points your employees have with your clients, potential clients and the community. Note the positive and negative impacts your employees could have and create a plan to mitigate against the risks and build upon the benefits.

- **Payroll Protocol:** Create your own Payroll Protocol, detailing what employees should do if there's an error in, or they have a concern about, their pay. Identify who they should notify, response timescales and provide an escalation procedure should they not be satisfied with the outcome or the timeliness of the response.

- **Employee Client Engagement Protocol:** Create your own Employee Client Engagement Protocol, ensuring adequate guidance is available for how employees should act, and what should and shouldn't be said in different situations.

Chapter Endnotes

11 Simon Sinek, *Start with Why*, Penguin, 2011.

12 Bob Burg, *Endless Referrals*, McGraw-Hill, 2005.

CHAPTER 10

Reputation

Payroll done with care,
Boosts trust, draws talent, clients,
Reputation thrives.

The reputation of your business, or you, as the business owner, can be destroyed by a single news story. Gerald Ratner's experience is a prime example. I was fortunate enough to meet him, albeit virtually, during a book and beer session hosted by a business contact of mine. He came across as humble, genuine and incredibly passionate about what he does. If you're unfamiliar with his story, I highly recommend finding out more and reading his book, *The Rise and Fall...and Rise Again*[13].

Gerald was the former CEO of Ratners Group, his family's jewellery business, and regularly gave keynote speeches due to the company's success. But one speech in particular dramatically altered the course of his life. On 23rd April 1991, at a conference for the Institute of Directors at the Royal Albert Hall, Gerald made a few off-the-cuff remarks about the products they sold, intended as a joke[14]. The press picked up on them, and within days, the story had spread across the country.

The consequences were swift and devastating. The value of Ratners Group plummeted by £500 million and the company was brought to its knees. Gerald brought in a chairman to stabilise the situation, but was ultimately ousted in November 1992. By 1993, the company had rebranded and closed 300 of its 2,500 stores. All from a few poorly chosen words.

What you say, and what others say about your business, matters enormously.

A strong reputation:

- attracts clients
- supports client retention
- strengthens client and employee relationships

- encourages top talent to join your business
- reduces recruitment costs
- reduces marketing costs.

Conversely, a bad reputation:

- deters clients
- weakens relationships
- drives away talented employees, leading to costly recruitment issues
- requires more spending on marketing
- spreads more quickly than a good reputation.

Your business reputation can be impacted in several ways:

- Word of mouth in your local community, eroding credibility and trust
- Social media, which can spread negative perceptions nationally and globally
- Local or national news coverage, which can amplify any negative stories
- Announcements from governing bodies or 'name and shame' campaigns
- Negative comments from influencers
- The actions of competitors.

In this chapter, I will explore the critical role payroll plays in shaping your business' reputation. I'll uncover how payroll practices directly impact employee satisfaction, retention and recruitment, which in turn influence public perception, client trust and stakeholder confidence. Through real-world examples and practical strategies, I'll highlight how a well-managed payroll system not only ensures legal compliance, but also boosts your brand image, helping you attract top talent and loyal clients. By the end of this chapter, you'll understand how safeguarding your reputation starts from within, by taking care of your employees.

Managing your business' reputation is crucial to its stability, longevity and profitability. Many forces, including external events or individuals, will try to disrupt your reputation. The best way to safeguard it is to be proactive, understanding the potential risks and mitigating them, wherever possible.

Remember, you can't control everything or how other people will act; it's how you react to situations as they happen that can show your true values.

The Role of Payroll in Reputation

Your business' reputation and its payroll practices are closely connected. Employee satisfaction, retention and recruitment all depend on consistently accurate and timely pay. Happy employees are productive, speak highly of your business and help build a positive public image. In contrast, unhappy employees, especially those who feel they've been treated unfairly, can quickly harm your reputation through negative comments, both online and offline.

How your business' reputation can be affected, can broadly be broken down into the following:

Employee Satisfaction, Retention and Recruitment

Paying your employees accurately and on time creates trust and loyalty. Fair compensation and clear communication boost employee satisfaction, influencing how employees talk about your business and, by extension, its reputation. In today's challenging recruitment landscape, a strong reputation makes it easier to attract and retain top talent. It also helps reduce recruitment costs and avoid losing key employees.

Payroll errors or issues can sour employee relations, leading to quicker frustration and damaging rants on social media or through word of mouth. On the other hand, employees who trust their employer are more likely to handle any payroll issues calmly, ensuring smoother resolutions.

Your employees are your business' most important asset. Looking after them not only makes your business a place where you and your employees want to work, but will boost your business' reputation, making clients and top talent want to work with you as well.

Stakeholder Relationships

Your reputation also affects how investors, suppliers and stakeholders view your business. Efficient payroll practices demonstrate financial stability, which builds confidence. A good reputation reassures investors and suppliers alike, while a bad one, regardless of financial performance, can deter future opportunities.

Public Image and Trust

Compliance and transparency in payroll, such as adhering to regulations and treating employees fairly, enhance your public image. People are more likely to trust and do business with one that is seen to value its employees, and that operates ethically.

Employer Brand

Your employer brand – the way you market your business to potential employees – is vital for attracting top talent. A positive reputation, shaped by employee experiences, influences this brand. Satisfied employees are more likely to recommend your business, and this goodwill is often reflected in client decisions too.

One thing you might consider implementing is a strong employee-focused reputation plan that can help project your values externally, and boost both recruitment and client attraction. This is where you can detail what values you want your business to be known for, developing that into an employee management structure and culture within your business, with the added gain of externally projecting a good image of your business as people-centred. This plan can also help you mitigate against the risk of brand damage through your relationships with your employees. The 3 action points from page 86 will be foundations for your employee-focused reputation plan, and using insight from this chapter you can now build upon them.

To build a strong employee-focused reputation plan, you need to prioritise respect, transparency, inclusivity within your business and plan for each of the potential touch points that your employees could have with the wider community to ensure you maintain a positive employer brand. You should consider and document your business' values and processes in relation to the different aspects of how you can create and maintain a happy workforce, and how you can express this to your community and clients. Every business is unique, so your plan will not be the same as any other business' plan. However, below are some suggestions on topics you might wish to include in your plan:

Open Communication: This is key, ensuring employees are informed and encouraged to share feedback. Have a section in your plan that focuses on how payroll will be communicated through your business. This can be from management to employees, or vice versa, giving clear guidelines on how payroll topics and changes should be communicated, including communication format, timeline, who should deliver the communication, who needs to be involved before the communication is issued, who authorises the information to be released and how the communication should be delivered (i.e. verbal, written, or a mixture of both).

Investing in Staff Development: Offering training and career growth opportunities shows genuine care for your employees' future. Document your business' strategy for investing in your employees, detailing items such as what your training budget is, an individual training matrix for each employee, the mechanisms for identifying training needs, and individual team members' strengths and weaknesses.

Promoting Work-life Balance and Mental Well-being: This can be done through flexible working policies, which help to retain talent. Detail what support and information you will provide to employees, where this information will be available, and who's in charge of keeping it up to date, distributing it and answering employee questions. There is no worse advertisement for your business than an employee who is stressed and exhausted.

Recognising Achievements: Publicly recognising your employees not only makes for great social media content, making your business shine by highlighting your employees' talents, knowledge and experience, but it also boosts morale, while creating inclusivity, creating a workplace where everyone feels they belong. Document what achievements you're going to recognise, aligning these with your business' goals and values. Keep a record of employee achievements and detail the methods for recognising achievements and what rewards employees will receive.

Regularly Measuring Employee Satisfaction: Acting on feedback ensures continuous improvement and helps you understand any issues that your employees face. This gives you the opportunity to fix these issues before they result in your employees moaning about them to their friends, family or your client. Document how you are going to measure employee satisfaction, how this changes over time and anything that impacts the level of your employees' satisfaction. Most importantly, detail what actions you're going to take, because knowing your employees' satisfaction level means nothing if you don't actively seek to improve it.

Together, these initiatives build trust and loyalty, creating a positive culture that attracts and retains the best talent. As well as planning for a happy workforce, you also need to mitigate against potential fallout. See below for a suggestion on how to build your plan to support you with this:

Employee-client Interactions: Your employees are the face of your business; the ones who will deliver your services, sell your products, and handle client queries and issues. A part of your employee-focused reputation plan needs to consider all the touch points your employees will have with your clients. Detail and communicate guidelines for employees on how you wish them to handle these interactions, what's acceptable to say and what's not, and how they should conduct themselves. Clearly outline the steps employees should take if they experience an issue with their pay or working conditions, ensuring they know how to resolve the matter swiftly and effectively. Provide a straightforward process for raising concerns, emphasising who the appropriate contact person is to handle such issues. This will help employees feel confident that their concerns will be addressed promptly, reducing the need to escalate the matter or discuss it with others. Ensure the communication is accessible and encourages a quick, direct resolution.

A potential client won't want to spend money with a business that doesn't look after its employees. This is for ethical reasons, priorities of the client and their confidence in your business being able to deliver a product/service that will fulfil their needs. Having an employee-focused reputation plan, where employee-client interactions are detailed and guidance given to employees on how these interactions should be handled, can support you in reflecting your values externally and, ultimately, draw clients to you.

Financial Stability and Operational Efficiency

Stable and consistent payroll practices signal financial security, reassuring investors, employees and clients alike. Good payroll management demonstrates sound cash management, a key indicator of a business' viability.

CSR (Corporate Social Responsibility)

How you treat your employees also reflects your commitment to CSR. Accreditations like Investors in People or Living Wage Employer can enhance your reputation by showing a clear commitment to fair pay and employee welfare. Even simple, everyday actions, such as treating employees with respect, build a responsible, people-focused brand.

Legal and Ethical Standing

Payroll is integral to compliance. There are plenty of laws and regulations that need to be adhered to when it comes to the pay and working conditions of employees. The timely dealing with payroll discrepancies and making the processes and procedures that payroll follow clear and transparent demonstrates your business' commitment to the ethical treatment of your employees.

Mistakes or oversights in payroll processes can lead to costly legal disputes, further damaging your reputation. For example, an employee who has been treated unfairly may take the employer to court to claim compensation. This not only costs the business money for defence, and for paying out to the employee, but also, whether the employer is found to be in the wrong or not, it damages the business' reputation. Most employee tribunals are held in public, meaning members of the public or press are able to attend, and the results of the tribunal are held on record, as case law, and can be used in future cases or law-making decisions, and free for anyone to access.

To illustrate this point, consider the Alabaster Ruling, which affects how SMP (Statutory Maternity Pay) is calculated when an employee receives a pay rise. This case, Michelle Alabaster v Woolwich plc (since taken over by Barclays Bank plc)[15] in 2004, was brought before the European Court of Justice and highlighted that the SMP regulations at the time did not fully comply with EU law. As a result, in 2005, the SMP regulations were amended to bring them in line with EU legislation. Previous case law also played a part in this decision, bringing the employers involved in those earlier rulings back into the spotlight. Every time a payroll professional has to recalculate SMP due to the Alabaster Ruling, we are reminded of the employers associated with it. While the employer in the Alabaster case did nothing wrong since it was the regulations that needed updating, they, along with the employers in previous related cases, continue to be cast in a negative light simply by virtue of their involvement in the legal process that led to this ruling.

Publicised cases, even if you win, can leave lasting reputational scars. They can be hugely damaging to a business and can have long-lasting effects.

Client Perceptions

Clients, both individuals and businesses, are influenced by the way your business treats its employees. Word of mouth, reviews, your website and social media interactions all contribute to their perception of you. First impressions matter, and happy employees are more likely to give clients a positive experience.

I've gone through the different aspects of reputation in relation to payroll. Let's now take a look at some of the ways your clients can see you and get to know who you are, and what you stand for.

Recommendations

Recommendations from friends, family or business contacts are incredibly persuasive when it comes to purchasing decisions. We all know that if someone we trust has had a positive experience with a business, be it through quality service or excellent customer care, we're more likely to choose that business over one we know nothing about. It reduces the risk in making that choice.

On the flip side, negative experiences travel much faster by word of mouth than positive ones. It's simply human nature. We're more inclined to vent about a bad experience to those around us when something has gone wrong.

It doesn't have to come from close friends or neighbours, or even a casual chat in the supermarket queue. It could be an online review, whether on Google, Yell, Facebook or LinkedIn. Word of mouth spreads quickly and can greatly influence how your business is perceived, both locally and nationally. The key factor driving these impressions is often your employees. So, it's essential that their focus remains on providing excellent customer service, not on issues like payroll errors or tax disputes. A happy, focused team will help you build a positive reputation for your business.

Website

Every business needs a website; a place where potential customers can find out what you do. Often, you'll have photos of your team on there, or if you're a smaller business, it might just be you as the face of the business. Whatever image you present on your website needs to match what potential clients experience when they get in touch. There's no point promoting a friendly, professional service if that's not what they encounter when they contact you.

If your employee is having a bad day or is unhappy with their working conditions or pay, they're unlikely to create the right impression. That first interaction is crucial. It can make all the difference in whether someone chooses to do business with you, and how much they'll spend. It also shapes what they'll say to their friends and family about your business.

Social Media Accounts

Social media policies for employees are now commonplace; something that wouldn't have been on the radar 10-15 years ago, but that are crucial in today's digital world. Picture this: an upset employee jumps straight on to Facebook to rant about being underpaid. They likely haven't waited to understand what happened or given time for the issue to be fixed. They're stressed, probably relying on that money for bills. Once the situation is resolved, perhaps it was just a misunderstanding, but the damage has already been done. That single post can have a devastating effect on your business, turning off potential customers who think, *If they can't pay their staff correctly, why would I buy from them?* It can also deter future employees, who see the post and think twice about joining your team.

The key takeaway is simple: even innocent rants from disgruntled staff can have a big impact on your business. That's why it's so important to have careful payroll processes and procedures in place to prevent issues that lead to bad press, whether it's through word of mouth or social media. Investing in your payroll is well worth it, not only for your employees who will be happier and more focused, but for your business' overall productivity and, crucially, its reputation.

News

At the start of the chapter I shared the story of Gerald Ratner and how one speech dramatically damaged his business' reputation. That was back in the 1990s, long before news was as readily accessible as it is today. Back then, it took days for a story to circulate; now, it can spread within minutes. With news available everywhere, on TV, in newspapers, online and across social media, there's no escaping it. Being aware of this and having strategies in place can help protect your business from the fallout of negative news coverage.

'Name and Shame' List

This one isn't as obvious. In Chapter 2 I mentioned HMRC's 'name and shame' list for NMW breaches (and they're considering doing the same for pension auto-enrolment). The list publicly identifies businesses that have failed to meet wage regulations. What impact would it have on your business and its reputation if you found yourself on that list?

The Power of Words

Ultimately, the story of Gerald Ratner is a reminder of the power of words. Whether it's you speaking on behalf of your business, or your employees, what is said and how it's perceived can have far-reaching consequences.

Reputation is about what you are known for. So, you need to decide what it is you want your business to be known for. Although a lot to do with reputation can seem out of your control, you do have a choice in the matter. Your payroll should be one of the first things you look at when assessing your business' reputation, as this is where a number of reputational issues begin.

By focusing on payroll and employee satisfaction, you can proactively protect your reputation and ensure your business is seen in the best possible light. Through thoughtful management, you can build a business and reputation to be proud of, starting with the way you treat your people.

Main Points

- Reputation management is crucial to the stability, longevity and profitability of your business.
- Happy employees, through improved productivity and profit generation, and unhappy employees, through low productivity impacting on profitability, stability and business operations, both impact your business' reputation.
- Your business' reputation and your employer brand have a massive impact on how easy you will find and recruit new employees, and how easy you'll bring new clients into your business.
- Transparency and compliance build trust with your employees, your stakeholders, your suppliers and your clients.
- The timely dealing with payroll discrepancies and making the processes and procedures that payroll follow, clear and transparent, demonstrate your business' commitment to the ethical treatment of your employees.

Action Points

- **Reputation Analysis:** Make two lists. One for ways your business reputation could be negatively affected; and the other one for positives. Plan how to safeguard against negatives and boost positives.

- **Employee-focused Reputation Plan:** Create a payroll reputation plan centred around employees, identifying employee touch point areas and how these should be handled.

- **Employer Brand:** Define what your employer brand is and what you want your business to be known for. Assess how it's perceived, identify areas for improvement and develop action plans. Ensure decisions and actions align with your desired brand image.

Chapter Endnotes

13 Gerald Ratner, *The Rise and Fall...and Rise Again*, Capstone, 2008.

14 Gerald Ratner speaking at the 1991 Institute of Directors Annual Convention, as viewed 18th February 2025: https://www.youtube.com/watch?v=Nj9BZz71yQE and Mark Peters, A Brief History, The Jewellers Guild, 2022.

15 European Union, Document 62002CJ0147, Judgment of the Court (Full Court) of 30 March 2004, Michelle K. Alabaster v Woolwich plc and Secretary of State for Social Security, Reference for a preliminary ruling: Court of Appeal (England & Wales) (Civil Division) – United Kingdom, Social policy – Men and women –

Equal pay - Pay during maternity leave - Calculation of amount – Whether to include a pay rise, Case C-147/02, https://eur-lex.europa.eu/legal-content/EN/TXT/?uri=CELEX%3A62002CJ0147

CHAPTER 11

The Value of Payroll to People

Payroll's steady hand,
Bridging people, pay and trust,
Success built on care.

When I worked for individual employers, I always reported to the Finance Manager or Director. There's been a long-running debate about which department payroll should sit under – Finance or HR? Payroll interacts closely with both, working with HR on the people side and Finance on the numbers. But there's a third option; that payroll should stand as its own department. Many in the payroll industry believe this should be the case.

For me, it doesn't really matter where payroll is placed on the organisation chart; it's just about structure and reporting lines. Each department has its role, but ultimately, they need to work together as one larger team for the business to function well.

What *does* matter to me is that payroll has a voice. Payroll needs to be part of leadership discussions, supporting businesses in making decisions that impact both people and numbers. Too often, we're brought into conversations far too late, once decisions have been made and implementation is under way. At this stage, we often spot risks, process gaps and system limitations that should have been considered much earlier. Without our input from the start, businesses miss out on our expertise, and we lose the chance to help ensure a smooth rollout.

Our expertise in compliance, systems and pay processes could prevent costly mistakes, ensuring employees are paid correctly, on time, and that the business stays compliant and mitigates risk. We understand the effects poorly managed changes can have on employees; from the queries we receive to the operational disruption they cause. Issues that could have been avoided if payroll was involved earlier.

In this chapter, I'll delve into the critical role payroll plays in effective people management and how it can be a powerful tool for motivating your workforce, boosting morale and enhancing overall job satisfaction. I'll explain how payroll goes beyond the numbers and acts as a strategic asset in retaining and engaging your employees. I'll provide examples of how payroll can strengthen the people side of your business, highlighting its impact on employee connection and loyalty. To round off, I'll discuss the vital relationship between you, your employees and payroll, demonstrating how prioritising both your people and your payroll not only creates a positive work environment, but also drives the long-term success of your business.

The Value Payroll Brings to Your People

Payroll is about more than just getting wages into bank accounts. It plays a crucial role in keeping employees happy, engaged and feeling secure.

Below are some of the ways payroll can really add value to your business.

Building Trust and Boosting Morale: Nothing damages morale like late or incorrect pay. A reliable payroll system builds trust, reassuring employees that their employer values them. When employees know their pay will be accurate and on time, they can focus on their work without distractions.

Increasing Employee Satisfaction: Smooth payroll processes contribute significantly to job satisfaction. Employees expect accuracy and timeliness as basic essentials, and when payroll delivers this, it builds trust. Providing access to clear, detailed payslips and up-to-date information about benefits, pensions and holiday entitlements also goes a long way towards boosting satisfaction.

Providing Transparency and Empowerment: A good payroll service offers employees clear information about their pay, tax and benefits. When employees understand how their pay is calculated and what they're entitled to, it creates trust and reduces confusion or frustration.

Ensuring Fair Pay for Effort: Employees want to feel their hard work is recognised, whether through a good salary, bonuses, overtime or commission. A well-run payroll system tracks these accurately, ensuring employees are fairly compensated, which helps them feel valued. Creating a Pay Reward Strategy for your business can help you become clear on how your pay will be structured, and how your employees will be rewarded for their efforts, whilst making sure it's cost-effective for your business. When you tie this in with your employee development strategy, how you will train and increase the knowledge/experience of your employees, it will encourage improvement and align employees with your business goals and values.

Aligning Pay with Performance: Payroll data is crucial for tracking performance-related pay, like bonuses or incentives. This ensures employees are rewarded for meeting goals, motivating them while aligning their efforts with the business' objectives.

Managing Benefits Smoothly: It's not just about salary anymore. Payroll handles everything from pensions and healthcare to gym memberships and cycle-to-work schemes. A smooth payroll operation ensures employees get the full value of their benefits, reducing admin headaches for the business.

Supporting Flexible Work Arrangements: As flexible working becomes more common, payroll needs to keep pace. Whether employees are part-time, remote or work irregular hours, payroll systems can adapt, ensuring everyone gets paid accurately, whatever the working arrangement.

Improving Communication: Payroll systems can sync with HR, giving employees easy access to information about holiday entitlement, sick pay or benefits. This level of transparency reduces admin for both employees and managers, freeing up time for more important tasks.

Promoting Employee Well-being: Payroll can play a role in well-being by offering early access to earned wages or salary advances for emergencies. Helping employees understand their financial data and reducing stress around pay can boost focus and productivity.

Ensuring Compliance with Statutory Requirements: From maternity leave to sick pay, payroll ensures employees receive the statutory pay they're entitled to. It's crucial for reducing legal risks and demonstrates the business genuinely cares about employee rights.

Creating Stability and Security: A well-run payroll system doesn't just pay employees; it creates a sense of stability. Employees who feel financially secure are more engaged and motivated, knowing they can rely on their employer to handle their pay and benefits smoothly.

Supporting Employee Retention: Payroll accuracy and transparency are key to creating a positive employee experience. When employees feel valued and respected through fair pay and clear benefits, they're more likely to stay, which reduces turnover and recruitment costs.

Helping Other Departments: Payroll doesn't work in isolation. Payroll supports HR by tracking employee leave, managing sick pay and handling bonuses, which frees HR to focus on strategic initiatives like employee development. Payroll also supports Finance by tracking payroll costs, explaining expenditure and projecting future costs. This integration is essential for a well-functioning business. For other departments, payroll helps keep employees focused on their work.

At its core, payroll is about looking after your people. It's not just about numbers on a payslip; it's about building trust, ensuring fairness and giving employees confidence in their financial security.

When payroll runs smoothly, it creates a positive work environment, where employees feel valued and motivated. This in turn adds value to your business.

The Evolution of People Management Through Payroll – Traditional v Strategic

Payroll has evolved from back office into a key function within people management, driven by technology, regulatory changes and a shift in workforce expectations.

What was once purely transactional, focused on entering and paying wages, has shifted to a strategic function. People management now involves employee engagement, talent development and creating a positive workplace culture.

Below are some ways in which payroll has evolved.

Automation: Payroll has transitioned from manual, paper-based processes to automated systems that handle tax, NICs, pensions and benefits in line with HMRC requirements. Automation has reduced errors and increased efficiency, freeing up payroll professionals to focus on more strategic work.

Impact of Legislation: Laws like the National Minimum Wage Act 1998[16], Working Time Regulations 1998, and Automatic Enrolment (as introduced under the Pensions Act 2008[17]), and many more, have transformed how payroll is managed. Staying compliant with these regulations is essential to protecting the business and ensuring employees are paid fairly.

Employee Self-service: Payroll systems can now enable employees to access payslips, update personal details and request leave through online platforms. This reduces admin for payroll teams and improves transparency for employees.

Flexible Working: Payroll has adapted to flexible working arrangements, accounting for part-time hours, remote working and various contractual agreements. This flexibility ensures employees are paid accurately, whatever their working setup.

Data Security and Compliance: With GDPR in force, payroll must ensure sensitive employee data is handled securely. Compliance with data security standards is a key responsibility, protecting both employees and the business.

Outsourcing Payroll: Many businesses now outsource payroll to third-party providers, ensuring compliance while reducing internal admin burdens. This option is increasingly popular, especially for SMEs (small and medium enterprises).

Data Analytics: Modern payroll systems provide valuable insights into workforce trends, helping businesses with financial planning and employee retention. Data-driven payroll allows leaders to make more informed decisions.

Payroll has transformed from a basic admin task to a critical function in people management and business strategy. Today, it supports employee engagement, compliance and data-driven decision-making, providing far more than just accurate pay.

Understanding the Value of Your People

In any business, people are the heart, and what pushes the business towards success. Whether it's a small local firm or a large multinational, the workforce is what drives performance, shapes business culture and delivers results. Recognising the true value of your people goes beyond job titles and performance metrics. It's about understanding the unique skills, perspectives and contributions each individual brings to the business and how they collectively drive success. Understanding and supporting your people is crucial.

Here's how payroll can play a key role in that support:

Engagement and Morale: Happy, motivated employees are more productive and loyal. When people feel valued and listened to, it reflects in their work. Building a strong connection with your staff by acknowledging their contributions and giving them the tools they need to succeed is essential.

Retention: Recruitment is expensive, so keeping hold of talented employees is a priority. People need to feel rewarded not just financially, but also in terms of development, work-life balance and career progression. The better you understand their needs, the more likely they are to stay.

Workplace Culture: People shape the culture of your business. A positive, inclusive culture creates a working environment where innovation thrives and teamwork flourishes. It's not just about perks; it's about creating an atmosphere where employees feel part of something bigger.

How Payroll Can Support People Management

Payroll might seem like a purely admin function, but as you can see, it plays a key part in supporting your people and, by extension, your wider business.

Below are a few ways payroll can support people management.

Accuracy and Trust: Payroll is one of the most direct interactions a business has with its employees. When people are paid accurately and on time, it builds trust and confidence in the employer. Errors or delays can lead to frustration, dissatisfaction and even a breakdown in that trust.

Transparency: Modern payroll systems allow employees to access their payslips and track their pensions or other benefits. This transparency helps employees feel in control of their finances and builds confidence that the business is taking care of their well-being.

Fair Compensation: Payroll ensures that people are paid fairly, in line with legal requirements like minimum wage or equal pay laws, but also with internal pay structures. Ensuring fair pay across teams, genders and roles supports a fair workplace and prevents disputes that can arise from perceived inequalities.

Employee Benefits: Payroll isn't just about the salary; it's about managing the full package: bonuses, sick pay, maternity/paternity leave, pensions and other benefits. A well-managed payroll system and process can easily handle these complexities, making sure employees are getting what they're entitled to, and supporting the overall employee experience.

Supporting Flexibility: In today's workforce, flexibility is more important than ever. Whether it's part-time schedules, flexible working times or remote working, payroll needs to be able to handle diverse working arrangements. For employees, this flexibility helps them maintain a healthy work-life balance. For employers, it's about offering the kind of working environment that attracts a modern workforce, while ensuring everyone is paid correctly and fairly.

Compliance and Security: There's also the legal side to consider. UK employment law is strict when it comes to payroll compliance, such as tax codes, statutory payments and pension auto-enrolment. A strong payroll system helps businesses stay compliant with employment law and HMRC regulations, ensuring no legal headaches down the road, while also keeping employees' personal data secure.

Payroll is more than just paying people. It's a critical part of people management that can strengthen the trust between employees and the business. When employees are confident that their pay is handled properly, they're able to focus on their work, knowing they're valued and supported. By investing in efficient, transparent, payroll systems and processes, you can support your people more effectively, enhance your employees' overall experience, keep your business running smoothly and make running your business easier on yourself.

How Does Payroll Integrate With and Support Existing Business SOPs?

Payroll plays a key role in supporting and integrating with your business' SOPs (Standard Operating Procedures), ensuring smooth operations across multiple departments.

Below are a few examples of how payroll aligns with existing SOPs, some of which I've touched on before.

Financial Management: Payroll syncs with accounting software to keep wage expenses, deductions and tax liabilities accurate. This ensures up-to-date financial records, aids budgeting, cash-flow management and financial reporting.

HR Management: Payroll integrates with HR systems to manage employee data, benefits and pay adjustments. It ensures smooth onboarding, promotions and leave management by keeping compensation aligned with employee status.

Compliance: Payroll calculates and files taxes, ensuring compliance with employment laws and minimising the risk of penalties. It helps your business stay in line with legal requirements such as minimum wage, overtime, benefits rules and much more.

Time-tracking: Payroll connects with time and attendance systems to accurately record hours worked and paid leave, ensuring employees are paid correctly and supporting workforce management.

Audit and Controls: Payroll provides a detailed audit trail, maintaining transparency for internal and external audits, and helping to spot discrepancies.

Performance Management: Payroll integrates with performance systems to align pay with employee performance, ensuring accurate bonuses and commissions, while motivating staff.

Budgeting and Forecasting: Payroll data feeds into financial planning, helping with budgeting, forecasting and resource allocation.

Employee Self-service: Some payroll systems can provide employee portals where staff can access payslips and manage their information, reducing admin tasks and payroll queries.

Risk Management: Security measures in payroll systems protect against fraud and unauthorised access, aligning with your risk management protocols.

IT and Data Security: Payroll ensures compliance with data security, backup and recovery protocols, safeguarding sensitive information.

Reporting: Payroll contributes to regular business reports, providing insights on costs, compensation trends and supporting decision-making.

Third-party Management: Payroll coordinates with benefits providers, ensuring accurate deductions and contributions to pensions and health insurance.

Payroll doesn't just manage wages; it ensures efficiency, compliance and strategic alignment throughout the business, making it essential for operational success.

Payroll as a Strategic Tool in People Management

Payroll is seen as an admin function, but it can be a strategic tool in people management. When used effectively, payroll supports a business' broader goals by contributing to employee satisfaction, retention and operational efficiency.

Here's how payroll can play a crucial role in shaping your business' people strategy:

Supporting Employee Retention: Payroll is directly tied to one of the most important aspects of an employee's work life - their pay. When employees trust that they'll be paid accurately and on time, it builds loyalty and reduces turnover. Moreover, by ensuring fair pay practices and providing clarity around pay such as bonuses, overtime and benefits, payroll helps employees feel valued and secure in their roles, reducing the likelihood that they'll look elsewhere.

Ensuring Fairness: A strategic payroll system allows businesses to ensure they are paying employees fairly across the board. By integrating payroll with HR data, businesses can regularly review pay scales, track salary trends and ensure there's no gender or diversity pay gap. This level of transparency builds trust and enhances your reputation as an employer who values fairness, contributing to a positive business culture.

Enhancing Employee Engagement and Motivation: Employees who feel fairly compensated are more likely to be engaged and motivated. Payroll systems can be linked to performance-based pay or bonuses, directly rewarding employees for their hard work and achievements. This can boost morale and motivation, encouraging employees to go the extra mile, knowing they'll be rewarded.

Data-driven Decision-making: Payroll systems provide valuable data that can inform strategic decisions in people management. This includes insights into overtime costs, workforce expenses, absence trends and salary benchmarks. By analysing this data, businesses can identify areas where they may be overspending or underpaying and make informed decisions on workforce planning, budgeting and even hiring needs.

Customising Employee Benefits: A modern payroll system doesn't just handle wages; it can manage a whole suite of employee benefits from pensions and bonuses to flexible benefits packages. These extras are increasingly important in today's job market, where employees expect more than just a salary. Payroll systems can offer flexibility in handling these packages, allowing businesses to tailor benefits to individual needs, which enhances job satisfaction and strengthens retention.

Improving Compliance and Reducing Risk: Payroll ensures that businesses remain compliant with the ever-changing landscape of employment law in the UK. From minimum wage requirements to pension auto-enrolment and tax regulations, payroll systems and personnel handle all these complexities, reducing the risk of costly fines or legal challenges. Staying compliant also demonstrates that the business values its legal obligations, which is key to maintaining a positive employer-employee relationship.

Building Financial Well-being for Employees: Payroll can also be a tool for supporting employees' financial well-being. Offering salary sacrifice schemes, like cycle-to-work programmes, enhanced pension contributions, or providing access to financial planning tools via the payroll platform, and explaining their pay to them, can make a real difference to employees. This shows the business is committed to their overall well-being, not just their work performance.

Facilitating Flexibility and Modern Working Arrangements: Today's workforce is increasingly diverse, with flexible and remote working becoming the norm. Payroll needs to be flexible too, adapting to different working arrangements like part-time schedules, remote work and varying shift patterns. By ensuring that payroll accurately reflects these varied work patterns, businesses can offer the flexibility employees want while maintaining accurate, efficient payroll processes.

Boosting Employer Branding: A strategic payroll approach enhances a business' reputation as a fair, transparent and caring employer. This helps attract top talent, particularly in competitive job markets where candidates are looking for employers who offer more than just a payslip. It attracts clients as well, through a positive outward reputation. A strong payroll system that offers timely payments, benefits management and clear communication adds to a business' attractiveness as an employer of choice.

Payroll is much more than just a way to pay your people; it's a strategic tool that influences retention, motivation, fairness and compliance. By aligning payroll with wider business strategies, businesses can create a supportive, transparent and efficient work environment that keeps employees engaged and loyal. When used strategically, payroll becomes a key part of people management, helping businesses achieve their long-term goals while taking care of their most valuable asset – their employees.

Examples of How Payroll Supports You and Your People

Payroll plays a vital role in supporting employers with their people, going beyond the mere transactional inputting of wage components.

Here are some practical case studies of how payroll helps businesses manage employees effectively:

Enhancing Employee Engagement and Retention:

Challenge: An employer who worked in the hospitality sector aimed to improve employee engagement and reduce turnover among its hourly workforce.

Solution: The employer leveraged payroll data to identify trends in employee retention linked to wage levels, overtime hours and scheduling consistency. The employer discovered that employees with more consistent schedules and better-managed overtime were more likely to stay longer.

Outcome: By adjusting scheduling practices and offering targeted raises to key employee groups, the employer was able to improve retention rates significantly. This not only reduced hiring and training costs but also enhanced the service quality to clients through a more experienced workforce.

Enhancing Employee Morale Through Transparency in Payroll:

Challenge: A fast-growing tech startup found that its employees were confused about how bonuses and commissions were calculated, leading to dissatisfaction and high turnover. The lack of transparency in payroll contributed to a sense of mistrust between employees and management.

Solution: The business adopted improvements to the transparency on its pay elements, offering detailed breakdowns of earnings, bonuses, commissions and other elements of pay for each employee. Clear guidelines were provided and communicated on bonus and commission structures.

Outcome: Employee trust in the payroll process increased, leading to a decrease in turnover. Employee surveys revealed that the workforce felt more confident in understanding their pay and benefits. The payroll team also noticed a reduction in queries, freeing up time for other tasks. Overall, the improved transparency led to higher employee morale and retention.

Promoting Work-life Balance:

Challenge: An office-based employer wanted to improve work-life balance for employees to align with its values of employee well-being.

Solution: By analysing payroll data, the employer identified employees who were consistently working overtime or not taking their holiday entitlement. The employer used these insights to promote flexible working hours, encourage time off, and offer better workload management.

Outcome: The approach helped improve employee satisfaction, reduced burnout and maintained a healthier work environment, which translated into higher productivity and lower employee turnover.

Restoring Reputation After Employee Discontent Impacts Client Relationships:

Challenge: A mid-sized consultancy business began to notice a decline in client retention and satisfaction. The cause became clear when several clients mentioned that employees had been openly discussing their dissatisfaction with pay and benefits during meetings. This not only reflected poorly on the business' professionalism but also raised concerns about the business' internal culture and stability. The business' leadership team realised that its employer reputation was at risk, potentially damaging both client relationships and its ability to attract top talent.

Solution: The leadership team took swift action, addressing the root cause of employee dissatisfaction. It organised a series of listening sessions with staff to understand grievances and communicate the financial realities of the business. A thorough review of the business' compensation and benefits structure was undertaken, ensuring it was fair and competitive. Additionally, the business introduced transparent communication channels and offered development opportunities to show investment in employees' growth. To address the immediate reputational impact, the business issued an internal policy discouraging any discussions of pay or benefits in client-facing settings. It also engaged directly with affected clients, reassuring them of the business' commitment to high standards and stability.

Outcome: Within a few months, employee morale had improved significantly due to the transparent approach and the positive changes in compensation and benefits. Client trust was restored through open communication, with several clients expressing appreciation for the business' proactive handling of the situation. As a result, client retention stabilised and the business' employer reputation rebounded, helping them attract skilled candidates in a competitive market.

Supporting Employee Development and Career Progression:

Challenge: A business struggled with unmotivated workforce, with low productivity. This created high turnover and impacted upon its profits.
Solution: The business turned to its pay structure for support in motivating the workforce, by creating a clear, documented Pay Reward Strategy. It did this by providing its employees with a simple pay progression and promotion structure. The business also improved its Talent Development Strategy and tied it into its pay strategy, thereby using payroll to manage promotions and salary increases. When employees complete training, or move up in the business, payroll adjusts salaries in line with these achievements. This helps employees see clear rewards for their development and the effort they put in, increasing satisfaction and retention.
Outcome: Employees understood what was required of them, what they would get out of the efforts they put in, and had support in achieving increased knowledge and experience in what they did. This motivated the employees and performance increased.

These case studies illustrate the impact that efficient payroll solutions can have on addressing complex people management challenges, from optimising workforce to improving employee satisfaction and well-being, ultimately improving business outcomes. You could do the same!

People, Payroll and You

People, payroll and employers are interconnected, and getting payroll right is essential for maintaining a smooth, productive relationship between employees and the business. Here's how they relate and how payroll plays a key role in supporting that connection:

People – The Heart of the Business

Your employees are your biggest asset. Whether it's the service to your clients, creative innovation or operational efficiency, your people are the ones making things happen. Keeping them happy, engaged and motivated is essential to business success. They expect fair pay, clear communication and support in all aspects of their working life, and that's where payroll steps in.

Employers – The Drivers of Strategy

As an employer, you set the strategy and direction of the business. Part of that strategy should be ensuring that your people feel valued, supported and fairly compensated. How you handle payroll, from paying employees on time to managing benefits, directly impacts how your people perceive you. A well-managed payroll system reflects your commitment to looking after your employees, building trust and loyalty.

Payroll – The Bridge Between People and Employers

Payroll is where everything connects. It's the mechanism that turns business strategy into tangible support for your people. It's not just about processing wages; it's about ensuring employees feel secure, valued and fairly rewarded for their efforts.

Here's how payroll supports both employees and employers:

Building Trust and Security: Payroll is the foundation of trust between employers and employees. Employees need to know they'll be paid accurately and on time. When payroll runs smoothly, employees feel secure, allowing them to focus on their roles without worrying about their finances. For employers, getting payroll right reduces stress, avoids unnecessary conflicts and helps maintain a positive work environment.

Supporting Fairness and Transparency: A transparent payroll system means employees understand exactly how their pay is calculated, from basic wages to tax deductions and benefits. For employers, it shows that you're committed to fairness and equity. This clarity helps avoid confusion or disputes and reinforces trust. It also allows businesses to ensure they're following equal pay laws, which is vital for creating an inclusive workplace.

Rewarding Effort and Performance: Payroll plays a key role in recognising and rewarding hard work. Whether it's tracking overtime, applying bonuses or managing commission-based pay, payroll systems ensure that employees are paid fairly for their contributions. For employers, this means keeping your people motivated and engaged, knowing their efforts are being properly recognised.

Managing Benefits and Well-being: Payroll is about more than just salaries. It's also responsible for managing the full range of employee benefits, such as pensions, healthcare, holiday pay and flexible working arrangements. For employees, these benefits are a key part of feeling valued. For employers, offering competitive benefits helps attract and retain top talent. Payroll systems keep everything running smoothly, ensuring employees get the full package they've been promised.

Ensuring Compliance: Payroll helps businesses stay compliant with UK regulations, from tax laws to minimum wage requirements and pension auto-enrolment. For employers, this is critical; getting it wrong can lead to fines, legal issues and damaged trust with employees. A reliable payroll system ensures all statutory requirements are met, giving peace of mind to both employees and employers.

Communication: Payroll acts as a communicator of employees' pay and benefits, from management and external parties, such as HMRC and the pension provider, to the employee. The effectiveness of this flow of information will determine the satisfaction of employees and, ultimately, their ability to focus on their work. For the employer, this means the difference between an unhappy workforce that are stressed about their financial situation, and a happy, engaged and productive workforce that knows their pay is being handled appropriately.

Reputation: If things go wrong with payroll, then the employees affected will express their dissatisfaction outwardly. This can result in a bad reputation for the employer and affects your employer brand.

At its core, payroll is the link between your people and your business. It's how you show your employees that they're valued, it's how you maintain fairness and trust, and it's how you support their well-being. For employers, payroll is a strategic tool that ensures compliance, drives employee engagement and, ultimately, helps your business thrive by keeping your people happy and secure. When payroll runs smoothly, everyone benefits; it's as simple as that.

Main Points

- Payroll is more than just numbers; it's about building trust, ensuring fairness and giving employees confidence in their financial security.
- Payroll has been transformed by data collection, automation, self-service and real-time reporting into an analytic tool for business leaders, and supports effective people management.
- Recognising the true value of your people goes beyond job titles and performance metrics. It's about understanding the unique skills, perspectives and contributions every individual brings to the business, and how they collectively drive success.
- By investing in efficient, transparent, payroll systems and processes, you can support your people more effectively, enhance your employees' overall experience and keep your business running smoothly.
- Payroll is a strategic tool that influences retention, motivation, fairness and compliance. By aligning payroll with wider business strategies, businesses can create a supportive, transparent and efficient work environment that keeps employees engaged and loyal.

Action Points

- **Payroll Integration:** Review how payroll aligns with and supports other business SOPs, ensuring smooth integration.
- **Pay Reward Strategy:** Develop a Pay Reward Strategy to motivate employees, linking it with your Talent Development Strategy for stronger outcomes.

Chapter Endnotes

16 The National Archives, Legislation.gov.uk, National Minimum Wage Act 1998, as viewed 15th February 2025: https://www.legislation.gov.uk/ukpga/1998/39/contents

17 The National Archives, Legislation.gov.uk, Pensions Act 2008, as viewed 15th February 2025: https://www.legislation.gov.uk/ukpga/2008/30/contents

Profit

Payroll is one of the largest investments for businesses, covering everything from salaries and wages to National Insurance, pensions and other employee benefits. When approached strategically, payroll can be a powerful tool to boost productivity and drive profitability. Aligning payroll with business objectives, through performance-related pay, bonuses and incentives, not only motivates employees but ensures their efforts are directly contributing to the business' success. By rewarding staff for their contributions, businesses can unlock higher performance, better align team goals with business priorities and, ultimately, maximise the return on their payroll investment.

However, when payroll is poorly managed, it can quickly erode profit margins. Overpaying staff, high employee turnover, mismanaging overtime or failing to track absenteeism can eat into the bottom line. Beyond wages, accurate payroll data provides critical insights into workforce costs, empowering businesses to make informed decisions on staffing levels and pay structures, which can enhance profitability.

Payroll also plays a pivotal role in cash-flow management. Meeting payroll on time, without fail, is essential; employees rely on it. This means businesses must ensure there are always sufficient funds available, even during leaner times or when unexpected costs arise. Failure to manage payroll effectively can create serious cash-flow challenges, particularly for smaller businesses or those with seasonal income fluctuations.

A well-managed payroll system, with forecasting tools, helps businesses anticipate upcoming payroll expenses and plan accordingly. This kind of foresight prevents cash shortages and ensures smooth operations. Mismanaging these obligations can disrupt cash flow and threaten financial stability.

Beyond its operational function, payroll is key to maintaining a business' financial health. Accurate and timely payroll is crucial for compliance with employment law, tax regulations and reporting requirements. Mistakes can result in fines, legal trouble and reputational damage, all of which can destabilise a business' finances. A strong payroll process safeguards against these risks, ensuring compliance and protecting the business from costly errors.

Integrating payroll data with financial systems enhances budgeting and forecasting accuracy, while linking payroll to performance helps inform workforce planning. Automation within payroll processes further improves efficiency, reduces errors and frees up time for strategic analysis, allowing businesses to focus on growth.

In this section, I'll explore the critical role that payroll plays in managing your costs and maximising profitability. First, I'll discuss the importance of understanding your numbers, including your current and future payroll expenses, as this is fundamental to controlling costs. Then, I'll look at how payroll impacts assets and liabilities, giving you a clear view of how it fits into your financial health. I'll also consider how payroll affects the overall value of your business, whether you're looking to grow, sell or transition the business to family successors. Finally, I'll examine how optimising payroll can contribute directly to profit maximisation, driving sustainable growth.

CHAPTER 12

Know Your Numbers

Costs flow like rivers,
Master payroll charts the course,
Steady growth awaits.

The term 'payroll' refers to the total amount of money that your business pays to your employees for their work and encompasses any benefits provided to your employees, and additional employer costs. The cost of your payroll is probably the most expensive cost in your business and will have a big impact on its stability, profitability and growth potential.

Knowing your payroll numbers will assist with cash-flow forecasting and help you understand your business' costs. When I talk about costs, I mean the human cost of a department within your business that produces a specific product or delivers a specific service. If you know how much things cost, you know how much you need to charge to be profitable. Also, knowing what your costs are means that you can work on reducing those costs by strategic planning, thereby reducing your outlays and increasing your profit margins. But it is only through the knowledge and understanding of your financial numbers that this is possible.

A point you'll hear a lot from your accountant, bookkeeper, business consultant or mentor is 'know your numbers.' Through this knowledge you can improve them and be in control of your business finances and financial stability.

In this chapter, I'll explore why payroll represents a significant cost, shedding light on the key factors that can either drive up or minimise these expenses. I'll then move on to demystifying payroll numbers, what they are and why they're crucial to your business. I'll examine the close link between payroll and effective financial planning, showing how a firm grasp of your payroll figures is essential for sound financial management. To round off the chapter, I'll explain why understanding your payroll numbers is not just important, but critical for running your business more efficiently, helping you avoid compliance pitfalls and financial missteps that could otherwise impact your bottom line.

Through this chapter I'll show how mastering your payroll can lead to smoother operations and greater long-term success.

Why Payroll is a Business' Biggest Cost

This section will delve into why payroll represents such a significant cost, breaking down its key components and demonstrating its impact on a business' overall budget. Grasping the full extent of payroll expenses is essential for sound financial planning and maintaining profitability.

Here are just a few key factors that substantially increase the human cost of running a business:

Labour-intensive Operations

Many businesses, especially those in the service sector, such as hospitality and tourism, rely heavily on human labour to operate. Employees are integral to providing services, and their compensation forms the bulk of the business' operational costs.

Employee Compensation Packages

On top of employee base salaries, hours and meeting your pension auto-enrolment responsibilities, you may provide compensation packages, including benefits such as health and dental insurance, bonuses and company cars. This keeps you competitive in the recruitment market and makes top talent want to work for you. These additional compensations can, however, add substantial extra cost to your business.

Keeping your employee compensation packages competitive varies considerably between professions, and therefore the financial implications to your business will heavily depend on the work you do. The more training, knowledge and experience, and the more technical or dangerous the work you require your employees to perform, the more you will need to compensate them, increasing your business' human costs of operation.

Legal and Regulatory Requirements

NMW, working laws and regulations determine the minimum amount an employee should be paid. Compliance with these laws ensures fair compensation to employees, but it also adds to the business' payroll costs.

Another legal and regulatory requirement for employers that brings significant cost to your business is that of pensions and auto-enrolment regulations. Careful financial planning, cash-flow forecasting and maintaining cash reserves are essential for you to meet all your employer regulatory requirements for the fair compensation and treatment of your employees.

Employer's NICs and Statutory Leave

Employers must pay employer's NICs based on employees' gross pay, and Class 1A employer's National Insurance on benefits provided to employees, to HMRC. In addition, employers must provide a number of statutory payments to their employees, if they meet the criteria, such as SSP (Statutory Sick Pay), SMP (Statutory Maternity Pay) and SPP (Statutory Paternity Pay). While there are currently reclaim options available for SMP and SPP, depending on your business' size, statutory payments still represent an added expense and further increase the overall cost of employing staff.

Attracting and Retaining Talent

As already mentioned, to attract and retain top talent that is skilled and brings value to your business, you need to provide good compensation packages. At the time of writing, the recruitment landscape is difficult for employers, with many struggling to find employees with the right training, skills and mindset. This is even more difficult when you're recruiting for a position that requires high skill, training, knowledge and experience, exacerbating the financial cost to your business.

The actual cost of recruiting staff adds to the business' expenses, especially when employee churn (the rate at which employees leave your employment and new employees begin working with you) is high, meaning that retaining employees is the most cost-effective approach to people management.

Overtime and Shift Fluctuations

This varies by industry, but for businesses that operate outside standard hours or experience high-demand periods, relying heavily on overtime pay or additional compensation for night and weekend shifts to incentivise employees can drive up payroll costs.

Training and Development

As an employer, it is essential to invest in your workforce. One, to ensure they are adequately trained to serve your clients in the best way; and two, for their personal and professional development, and job satisfaction. Training and developing your employees not only requires a significant time investment but also adds considerable financial strain, further increasing the overall expense of managing your workforce.

Geographical Pay Variations

Where an employee lives can affect the amount of compensation they will expect. For example, someone living in London will have higher costs of living than someone in another part of the UK. If your business needs to operate in an area that has a higher cost of living, then you'll need to adjust your payroll budget according to the geographical market standards.

Payroll Numbers and Why They Matter

Understanding key payroll numbers is essential for ensuring accuracy, compliance and sound financial management. Accurate payroll processing ensures employees are paid fairly and on time, while also keeping the business compliant with tax and employment laws. Missteps can lead to fines, legal action and damaged employee relationships, affecting morale, turnover and your reputation as an employer.

Here are some important payroll terms and why they matter:

Gross Pay: The total pay before deductions, forming the basis for calculating taxes, NICs, pensions and other deductions. Tracking gross pay helps ensure proper budgeting for workforce costs.

Net Pay: An employee's take-home pay. Ensuring deductions are correct is crucial for maintaining employee satisfaction and avoiding pay discrepancies.

PAYE Tax: Income tax deducted from wages and paid to HMRC. Accurate calculation and timely submission are legal obligations, with errors potentially leading to penalties.

NICs: Contributions from both employer and employee towards state benefits. Timely and accurate payments are essential for managing cash flow and ensuring employee entitlements.

Pension Contributions: Payments into employee pension schemes, under auto-enrolment rules. Employers must ensure compliance to avoid fines from The Pensions Regulator.

BIKs (Benefits in Kind): Non-cash benefits such as company cars or private health insurance, which are taxable and have NIC implications for the employer.

Staff Turnover Rates: Payroll can track how frequently employees leave, offering insights into satisfaction and potential issues with pay or workload. High turnover is costly and may signal deeper business problems.

Payroll As a Percentage of Revenue: A key metric that shows how much of your revenue is going towards payroll costs.

Understanding this percentage helps ensure sustainable margins and identify areas for improvement.

Knowing your payroll numbers not only keeps you compliant and avoids costly errors, but also helps you manage cash flow, forecast expenses and build a strong, well-run business that employees trust and want to be part of.

Employer Costs

Understanding your total payroll costs per employee is essential for financial forecasting and budgeting. When assessing your current employee costs or planning to hire, there are six key payroll numbers every employer needs to consider. I've mentioned some of these already, but it's important to be clear of what exactly is impacting on your bottom line.

Gross Pay: The base salary agreed on with the employee. You need to ensure it fits within your payroll budget and is competitive enough to attract talent.

Employer's NICs: On top of the employee's salary, employers must pay NICs, so factor this into the total cost of hiring.

Employer Pension Contributions: Auto-enrolment requires employers to contribute to employees' pensions. Be aware of the minimum contribution and include it in your overall payroll plan.

BIKs: Non-cash perks, like company cars or private healthcare, must be accounted for in payroll and involve additional NIC costs for the employer.

Overtime and Bonuses: If the role includes potential overtime or performance bonuses, these need to be factored into both gross pay and your wider payroll budget, including NICs and pension contributions.

Apprenticeship Levy: If your annual payroll exceeds £3 million (at the time of writing), you'll be liable for the Apprenticeship Levy. Small business owners should keep this in mind as the business grows.

By keeping track of these costs, you can hire smartly and manage payroll effectively, ensuring your business stays on top of financial obligations while remaining competitive.

Recruitment Costs

Employer recruitment costs and payroll are closely linked, as hiring new talent has a direct impact on the business' finances. Recruitment costs go beyond just advertising a job. When you factor in time spent by HR teams, interview processes, recruitment agencies and onboarding, the price can add up quickly. Here's where payroll ties in.

Firstly, when recruiting, employers need to budget for the new hire's wages, which impacts overall payroll costs. You also need to factor in NICs, pensions and any benefits or perks the employee is entitled to, as mentioned. This isn't just about what the employee sees on their payslip; it's the full cost of employing them, which includes everything from tax deductions to BIKs.

On top of that, there's the cost of covering gaps in staffing while the recruitment process is ongoing. Whether it's paying overtime to existing employees or bringing in temporary workers, these costs need to be managed carefully in payroll to avoid unexpected budget overspends.

Finally, retention also plays a big part. The costs can soon mount up when recruiting, from the cost of advertising the post, the fee for the recruitment agency (if you use one) to the cost of cover while the recruitment process goes on (which often takes a while), and training costs for your new starter. If you're paying good money to recruit the right people, but then losing them due to poor payroll practices like mistakes with pay, missed deductions, poor communication or unclear benefits, it just means higher turnover and more recruitment costs. So, by keeping payroll efficient and transparent, you're also investing in long-term employee retention, which saves on those expensive recruitment cycles.

Financial Planning

Effective financial planning is closely tied to understanding your payroll. Knowing your payroll numbers is key to maintaining healthy cash flow and long-term sustainability. It's not just about paying salaries; it's about forecasting costs, managing budgets and ensuring you can support your team while growing your business. With proper financial planning around payroll, you'll have a clear picture of your outgoings, allowing you to plan ahead, make informed decisions and avoid nasty surprises. Smart payroll planning keeps your finances in check and your business on track.

Below are some of the main aspects to consider.

Cash Flow and Forecasting

A positive cash flow allows you to pay off your suppliers, pay your wages and keep the business afloat. Having a strong forecast of future business expenses allows you to plan better, giving you potential cash that can be reinvested back into the business. It can allow you to pay up front for items you need to purchase, meaning you could potentially pay less as you don't need credit. This saves your business in the long run and gives you more money for the benefit of you and your business. Payroll has a big part to play in accurately forecasting your business' numbers. A good understanding of your payroll demographics now and what might be required in the future can support you in making more informed and better decisions for your business.

Accurate payroll numbers are essential for forecasting cash-flow needs. Understanding upcoming payroll expenses helps businesses plan for future cash needs and avoid cash shortfalls.

Regular Cash Outflows

Payroll represents a substantial and regular flow of cash out of the business. Timely and accurate payments to employees, HMRC, the pension provider or other third parties is essential, and managing the outflow of cash is crucial for maintaining a healthy cash flow. Ensuring on-time payments keeps employees happy and focused on their work, and keeps your business in line with regulatory requirements, avoiding penalties and fines for non-compliance.

Cash Reserves

Understanding your current and future numbers, including bank balances, costs and revenue predictions, helps you maintain enough cash reserves to keep the business running in case of unexpected events. A prime example of this is Covid-19 and all the restrictions that were put on everyone. Businesses were provided support by the government to help afford their wages bill through the furlough scheme, but this didn't cover all the wages, nor all the other business costs. Even if the business is not legally allowed to operate, employee contracts and payments still need to be honoured.

Maintaining sufficient cash reserves to cover payroll is critical. Your employees must get paid, no matter what, and on time.

To meet their wages bill, some employers may look to financing during cash-flow shortages. This could involve short-term loans or other lines of credit, which come with their own costs and impact on cash flow. This may not be necessary, with good financial planning. Knowing your numbers and having good estimates of future costs based on solid, detailed, accurate and relevant information, means you can budget for future costs and ensure you have enough cash reserves to see you through.

Planning and Budgeting

Accurate payroll numbers help in forecasting employee costs, managing cash flow and making informed financial decisions within your business. They allow for budgeting and planning for future costs, projects and growth, to ensure that enough cash reserves are in place to support the ongoing operations of your business.

Cash-flow planning and cash reserves are extremely important to the financial stability of your business. This was highlighted during the Covid-19 outbreak, with a lot of good businesses failing and closing their doors due to a lack of good financial understanding and planning.

Demographics

So, how do you know and analyse your payroll numbers? By starting with your employee demographics, as mentioned in Chapter 8. These are statistics and information that payroll collects and reports on, such as age, gender, ethnicity, education, working location, length of service, position specifications and more. It can even be the knowledge, experience and skill set your employees possess, to perform their job.

Remember, the demographics of your business are affected by the type of industry you're working in and the type of duties your employees are required to perform. An employee performing simple tasks, with minimal training or experience, will be compensated differently and will have different demographic requirements, compared to a position requiring highly skilled and experienced personnel.

To illustrate this point, take a small café worker and an aircraft pilot. For a café worker you need an employee to take orders to give to the kitchen, to take the order to the customer's table, clean tables, wash dishes etc. There's not a lot of training required, and previous experience is not essential for the role. This is likely to be a NMW role or tracking a little above. However, an aircraft pilot requires years of training, they need to gain a university degree and are required to notch up many hours of flying time before they graduate to be a pilot. Their pay will be much greater.

A café worker is more likely to be younger than an aircraft pilot due to experience, training required and pay expectations. So, to understand your payroll costs, you need to first understand the demographics of the roles you need to fill within your business, and those of the employees already on your payroll. You need to know the role requirements to run your business effectively. To understand the current and future requirements allows you to budget and more accurately analyse cash flow for your business.

Demographics are valuable for businesses in assessing current and future payroll costs. Since they are specific to your business, your demographic mix will be unique and will evolve as employees join and leave, and as the business grows and changes. This mix is influenced by what your business does and where it operates, reflecting the demographics of your workforce. This all helps you understand your workforce and how they may evolve over time and as the business grows. With this information and understanding comes control – control of the costs and therefore maintenance of a positive cash flow and ample cash reserves should events such as Covid-19 happen again. Rather than reacting to the events as they happen and finding you are not in a good position to cope with them, you're planning ahead.

Take a look at your business' demographics; what they are currently and what they will need to be in, say, 5 or 10 years' time. If you have a workforce that is ageing and you have a number of employees close to retirement age, you need to know and plan for that now, not when it happens. I also suggest you review your demographics if you're looking to develop a new product or service, or if you want to take your business in a different direction. Consider this: Do you have the right skills in your business now for that new product or service, or do you need to hire for them? If so, what skills do you need? Demographic analysis will help you plan for the future and have a better understanding of your payroll costs.

Are You Ready to Hire?

When taking on employees, it's not just the wages and other payments you need to consider (which I have already outlined in this chapter); you also need to take into account other costs like computers and software, desks and equipment, insurances, policies and contracts. It's important to know all the actual or potential costs in advance, then you can plan accordingly.

I mentioned earlier that when I was ready to take on my first employee, I started by hiring a part-time employee. Why? This gave me support to assist with day-to-day running tasks, but minimised the initial wage cost. It allowed me to get my foot on the employer ladder, without putting the business at more risk than was required. It allowed me to move on quicker to hiring a second employee, also part-time. This gave me two employees, quicker than if I had hired full-time, meaning I had cover for sickness/holidays. It meant not all the work would come back on me, and I was able to more easily manage the risks involved. Taking on part-time employees meant I could manage the costs of hiring and gave some flexibility.

Whether you're about to embark on your employer journey or you're already an established employer, analysing your payroll setup and costs can provide huge benefits to your business, allowing you to manage this big cost. Understanding your payroll numbers gives control, as well as the advantages of being able to plan better and minimise your costs, where possible.

Hiring is expensive and is often a task a lot of us get wrong. It's hard to anticipate how an employee is going to work out, or how you and your business are going to work with someone else helping. It takes time to become accustomed to being an employer and know what it is your business needs. Often, the knowledge and understanding of what you need, how it's going to work and how you are going to cope with being a manager, only comes through trial and, a lot of the time, error. This is absolutely fine, as long as you learn from your experiences. But this trial-and-error approach can get costly, with costs of recruiting and finding an employee, the time and resources involved in training them, the costs of equipment and insurances required, the cost of their wages and, if it doesn't work out, the cost of starting the process all over again. This is why seeking expert advice, planning and knowing the potential costs are crucially important.

I'll highlight why it's important to plan before hiring by leaning back on an example I gave in Chapter 8; of an employer I worked with who was in the process of developing his product and was caught out by Covid-19. As mentioned, when he started out building his team, he wanted to be an employer who paid his employees well. A commendable approach, and great for his employer brand and business' reputation. He gave good salaries and increased employer pension contributions.

The issue was that his product hadn't launched yet, leaving him entirely dependent on bank funding. The funding had been agreed and was all in place, but Covid-19 hit. Along with many other businesses at the time, the bank pulled his funding. Heartbreakingly, the employer needed to let go of all his employees, as he simply couldn't afford to pay them.

If he'd focused on payroll cost analysis, knew his payroll numbers, planned and forecasted carefully, and been more conservative with salary and benefits until his product launched and the business was established, he might have survived until the banks resumed lending.

We all want to be that great employer, but knowing your payroll numbers and using employee demographics to estimate future costs is the difference between a business that may suddenly stop trading and a business that's stable and profitable. In this example, the employer was trying to do well for his employees and his business, his intentions were in the right place and his employees ended up out of a job, impacting his business' reputation, his employer brand and, ultimately, halting business operations.

Reporting and Analysis

The data payroll produces and the records payroll keeps, provide valuable insights into the human costs of business. You can analyse productivity, the cost of particular products, services or projects, and other important measures. Every business is unique, so being able to drill down into the financial cost of your business provides a good understanding of your costs, as well as being able to estimate, and predict, how your costs will evolve with your business over time.

The more accurate and meaningful the information and numbers used for analysis, the more informed your decision-making will be, and the more you can operate strategically, rather than reactively.

There are many reporting requirements in business, but, for an example, one of the biggest reporting requirements for payroll is that of hours worked. These records not only keep your business compliant, allow for correct payments of hours to employees and calculations for holiday pay, they also allow for the working patterns within your business to be analysed. This allows you to manage your workforce more effectively. But this is not an area that all businesses are good at. I come across businesses every week that don't have strong records of when their employees work, even though this is a legal requirement for things like the NMW regulations, as discussed in Chapter 2. So, a little plea from me: please keep good records of working hours for your employees; it's fundamental for compliance and accurate payroll calculations.

Accurate Payments

Payroll deals with lots of numbers and they all need to be transferred, organised and flow into accurate payments, with payments made to employees, to HMRC, to pension providers and to other third parties. Any of these numbers could be lost, confused, typed the wrong way, misinterpreted, picked up wrong or forgotten about. But these numbers need to be collated, recorded and ordered correctly. Whether you're calculating hours due, prorating salary for a new starter or leaver, or how much tax needs to be deducted; whatever it is, precise calculations are crucial for maintaining employee trust and satisfaction.

Seasonal Fluctuations

Many businesses experience seasonal fluctuations, particularly in industries such as retail, tourism and hospitality. For businesses with seasonal fluctuations in revenue, managing payroll during off-peak times can be challenging. Planning for these fluctuations and managing cash flow accordingly are crucial.

During the Covid-19 pandemic's first lockdown, many seasonal businesses that experienced their peak revenue during the summer, went from winter to winter, while most of the population were locked down in their homes during the summer period. It is during these peak-revenue-generating months that these types of businesses build up the revenue reserves needed to see them through their off-peak periods. Without the revenue-generating season, these businesses were put under a lot of pressure, with a number of them needing to close their doors as their cash flow and cash reserves could not withstand the strain. If you have a business like this, then your cash-flow forecasting and cash-reserve management needs even more care and attention.

Scalability

As your business scales, payroll becomes more complex and harder to manage. With more employees comes the need for a robust payroll system that can handle increased data, changing pay structures and various payment types. If your payroll processes aren't built to grow with your business, you'll risk errors, inefficiencies and potential compliance issues. Proper payroll management is crucial for keeping your operations running smoothly as you expand, ensuring you can focus on growth without the headaches of payroll problems.

Business Expansion

With business growth comes the need for more staff. Unlike some operational costs that may decrease with economies of scale, payroll often increases steadily, or rapidly, as you expand. Financial planning is crucial to keep on top of these rising human costs and to ensure that your business growth remains sustainable.

Employee Growth

As your business grows, so does the complexity of your payroll. More employees means more data to manage, and without accurate numbers and efficient planning, things can quickly spiral out of control. Ensuring your payroll processes can scale smoothly is key to handling new hires, changes in pay structures or different types of payments without any hiccups.

Payroll Numbers Are Important

Your payroll numbers are a fundamental part of your payroll process. They ensure accuracy and compliance. They enable good financial management, tax reporting, benefits administration, record-keeping, timekeeping, reporting, consistency, error reduction and the platform for scalability. These factors all collectively contribute to the smooth and efficient operation of your payroll.

Payroll impacts on the cash-flow reserves, outflows, forecasting, budgeting and planning within your business. Careful management of your payroll costs and seasonal fluctuations is essential to maintain a healthy financial status and ensure the continuing financial stability of your business.

Main Points

- With workforce expenses being the largest portion of your business budget, payroll plays a crucial role in your business' financial stability and long-term viability.

- Retention plays a big part in managing payroll costs. Spending significant money to hire the right people, only to lose them due to poor payroll practices, means higher turnover and increased recruitment costs.

- Payroll is not just about paying salaries; it's about forecasting costs, managing budgets and ensuring you can support your team while growing your business. Knowing your numbers gives you control and peace of mind.

- Payroll has a big part to play in accurately forecasting your business numbers. A good understanding of your payroll demographics can support you in making informed and improved decisions for your business.

- As your business grows, the demand for more employees rises. Unlike some operating costs that may decrease per unit with economies of scale, payroll costs typically increase linearly or can even grow exponentially, meaning they rise faster as your business expands.

Action Points

- **Employer Cost Analysis:** Calculate your total payroll costs, per month and per year, breaking down each contributing factor.
- **Cash-flow Forecast:** Create a 12-month payroll cash-flow forecast.
- **Demographic Cost Analysis:** Analyse your current payroll demographics and predict what your business will need in 5 and 10 years. Regularly review and update these projections.

CHAPTER 13

Assets and Liabilities

In payroll's balance,
Liabilities dissolve,
When assets are seen.

Hiring an employee is not merely adding a resource but making an investment that can drive your business forward. Their skills, knowledge, dedication and, ultimately, their productivity, are essential for achieving your business' strategic objectives and long-term success.

Yes, an employee's return on investment is unknown, hard to predict and does come down to the productivity of the individual that works for you. An employee's productivity can fluctuate, as the efficiency in how we work is influenced greatly by many external factors. But, ultimately, the return you get from your employees is in your hands; it's about how you view and manage them. If you see them as a liability, a burden or a drain on your financial resources, that's exactly what they'll become. But if you see your employees as valuable assets, key to your business' development and growth, and manage them accordingly, they'll rise to that expectation and drive your success.

Payroll plays a crucial role in tipping the balance between seeing your employees as valuable assets or as liabilities. It's often viewed as a liability itself, but when handled correctly, payroll becomes a powerful asset that can drive real value. How you approach and manage payroll will determine which side of the scale your business tips towards. By strategically managing payroll and continuously investing in your people, you can unlock their full potential, fuelling long-term business success. This not only helps you balance costs and rewards but also boosts employee satisfaction and performance.

In this chapter, I'll explore the concept of employees as both liabilities and assets to your business, with a focus on how payroll plays a crucial role in determining which side of the balance your workforce falls on. I'll examine the financial, legal and operational risks employees can pose, from rising costs to compliance challenges and productivity issues, and how payroll processes can either exacerbate or mitigate these risks. I'll also discuss how employees, when supported by effective payroll processes, can be transformed into valuable assets, driving productivity, innovation and growth. By delving into both sides, you'll gain a deeper understanding of how optimising payroll management can turn a potential liability into a strategic advantage, ultimately helping you build a stronger, more resilient and profitable business.

Liabilities

Employees can be a liability to your business in various ways, primarily due to costs, risks and potential negative impacts on your business' operations and reputation.

Below are some of the key aspects of payroll that can influence, enhance or disrupt the balance between employees as a liability or employees as an asset. These elements play a crucial role in optimising your employees' efficiency, controlling your business' costs and ensuring overall financial stability.

Financial Costs:

- **Salaries and Benefits:** The ongoing costs of salaries, wages, benefits and other compensation can be substantial.
- **Training and Development:** Expenses related to training and upskilling your employees, especially if employee turnover is high, can be significant.
- **Recruitment and Hiring:** The process of recruiting, hiring and onboarding new employees involves considerable time and investment.

- **Offboarding:** Redundancy and severance agreements can be significant costs.

Legal and Compliance:

- **Employment Law Issues:** Employees can bring legal action against your business, for issues such as wrongful termination, discrimination, harassment or wage disputes.
- **Regulatory Compliance:** Failure to comply with employment laws, health and safety regulations and other legal requirements can result in fines and penalties.

Productivity and Performance:

- **Low Productivity:** Underperforming employees can drag down overall productivity, efficiency and affect workforce morale.
- **Absenteeism and Turnover:** High rates of absenteeism and employee turnover disrupt operations, morale, and increase recruitment and training costs.

Workplace Conflicts and Morale:

- **Conflicts:** Interpersonal conflicts among employees or between employees and management can create a toxic work environment and reduce overall productivity.
- **Low Morale:** Poor management practices, lack of engagement or inadequate compensation can lead to low employee morale, affecting performance and retention.

Reputation and Brand Damage:

- **Negative Publicity:** Misconduct, unethical behaviour or poor client service by employees can damage your business' reputation (mentioned in Chapter 10).
- **Social Media Risks:** Negative comments or actions by employees on social media can quickly harm the business' public image.

Operational Risks:

- **Errors and Mistakes:** Human error can lead to costly mistakes, defective products or substandard services.
- **Dependence on Key Employees:** Over-reliance on key employees, without adequate succession planning, can be risky, if those employees leave or retire.

Security Risks:

- **Data Breaches:** Employees can inadvertently or maliciously cause data breaches, leading to significant financial and reputational damage.
- **Theft and Fraud:** Employees might engage in theft, embezzlement or fraud (as in the embezzlement story I told in Chapter 2), which can result in financial losses.

Adaptability Challenges:

- **Resistance to Change:** Employees resistant to new technologies or processes can slow down innovation, adaptation and progress.

- **Skills Gaps:** Employees lacking necessary skills can hinder business growth and responsiveness to market changes.

While employees are essential for your business' success, managing these potential liabilities requires careful planning, effective management practices and a proactive approach to mitigate risks.

Assets

Employees and payroll can be amongst the most valuable assets a business can have. Skilled and motivated employees drive productivity, innovation and success, while the payroll system ensures they're compensated accurately and on time, which builds trust and loyalty. Together, they form the backbone of a thriving business, with employees contributing their time and talents, and payroll representing the business' commitment to its people. When managed well, these elements create a strong, sustainable foundation for growth.

Below are some examples of employees as assets, supported by strong payroll processes and procedures.

Productivity and Performance:

- **Operational Efficiency:** Skilled and well-trained employees are key to running a smooth and efficient operation, boosting productivity and cutting business costs. By having a reliable system in place, tasks are completed with greater accuracy, deadlines are easier to meet, and employee queries are resolved promptly. This allows your team to focus on driving operational efficiency across the business.

- **Quality of Work:** High-performing employees produce quality work, in less time, which positively impacts the business' reputation and supports client satisfaction. A payroll process that reduces employees' stress and keeps their focus on their work will be able to produce higher-quality work.

Innovation and Growth:

- **Creative Solutions:** Employees bring diverse, fresh perspectives and ideas that can lead to innovative products, services and processes. Payroll demographic analysis – to ensure diversity within the workplace – and the right employee compensation packages give the space, in your employees' minds, for creativity. Creativity that enhances the efficient running of your business, and the quality and functionality of your products or services, making your business more desirable to your clients.
- **Continuous Improvement:** When employees are engaged in their work, they often seek ways to improve and optimise business operations, which drives growth, performance and, ultimately, your business' success. Using continuous improvement enhances the quality of your payroll process, maximising the human resources within your business, and manages your business' costs and financial security.

Client Relationships:

- **Service:** Employees are the face of your business. They play a crucial role in building and maintaining client relationships through excellent service. A well-run payroll will reduce the likelihood of your employees complaining, potentially to clients, about their employment and pay issues, freeing them to provide that five-star service.
- **Loyalty:** Satisfied clients, through positive interactions with employees and simple/straightforward processes derived by innovation, will spend more with your business. Not only that, they'll tell other people – their families, their friends, the lady in front of them at the supermarket checkout – all of which builds a positive reputation for your business. If your payroll processes result in accurate, on-time payments to employees, with good communication, then trust is built, and your employees will stick around. This not only reduces your recruitment costs, but keeps trained and knowledgeable employees – who are able to provide the best service to your clients – within your business.

Culture and Morale:

- **Positive Environment:** A motivated and cohesive workforce creates a positive business culture, which can enhance overall employee morale and job satisfaction. This makes the working environment more conducive to collaboration and innovation. Trust is an important factor in creating a positive working culture. A well-managed payroll process can support an environment where trust is built and maintained.
- **Employee Retention:** A strong, supportive culture helps retain top talent, reducing employee turnover and associated

recruitment costs. The trust built through a strong payroll process, that has your employees at the heart, will retain your employees and the talent within your business more effectively.

Brand and Reputation:

- **Reputation-building:** Employees who are proud of their workplace can become brand ambassadors, promoting the business positively, both online and offline.
- **Talent Attraction:** A strong employer brand attracts high-quality candidates, further strengthening the business with the right skills and experience.

Operational Knowledge:

- **Operational Memory:** Long-term employees hold valuable operational knowledge and experience gained over time, which can be crucial for training new hires and maintaining continuity.
- **Problem-solving:** Experienced employees can quickly address and solve problems based on their deep understanding of the business' operations and needs.

Adaptability and Resilience:

- **Flexibility:** A well-trained workforce can adapt to changes in the market, technology and business strategies, helping the business remain competitive.

- **Crisis Management:** In a time of crisis, dedicated employees can be a key resource for navigating challenges and ensuring business continuity.

Financial Impact:

- **Revenue Generation:** Employees directly contribute to generating revenue. Through sales, production and service, even those employees in back-office positions contribute to revenue generation through supporting employees who deal with clients directly, or with those who produce the products.
- **Cost Management:** Effective employees can contribute to cost savings, through efficiency and innovation.

Employees are not just a resource; they are an investment that drives your business forward. Their skills, knowledge and dedication are essential for achieving the business' strategic objectives and long-term success.

Balancing the assets and liabilities associated with employees and payroll is crucial for maintaining a healthy, productive and profitable business.

Payroll – From Liability to Asset

You've seen how payroll can enhance the employee experience, but how do you shift the perception of payroll from a liability to an asset? While this may not be achievable from an accounting perspective, you can certainly change how payroll is managed and viewed within your business to extract more value. Below are some key areas where payroll can impact the balance between employees as liabilities or assets. These factors are vital for optimising workforce efficiency, controlling costs and maintaining financial stability.

Compensation Structure: A well-designed pay structure can motivate employees, boosting productivity and lowering turnover.

Benefits Management: Offering competitive, tailored benefits that suit employees' lifestyles can attract top talent and improve satisfaction, leading to higher retention rates.

Invest in Employee Development: Skilled, engaged employees are more productive, generate more business and improve your bottom line. Payroll then becomes an investment in future value.

Link Payroll to Performance: Introducing performance-based pay or bonuses ties payroll outflow to measurable outcomes or KPIs (Key Performance Indicators). When employees know that hitting targets leads to rewards, productivity rises, making payroll a tool for driving higher returns.

Retention and Job Satisfaction: High turnover makes payroll feel like an endless expense with little long-term benefit. Focus on retention and satisfaction strategies to ensure that payroll is spent retaining high-value staff, reducing recruitment and onboarding costs.

Optimise Payroll with Technology: Inefficient payroll systems drain time and resources. Streamlining payroll with automated systems can save on admin costs, reduce errors and help turn payroll from a burden into a smooth, cost-effective process that supports growth.

By shifting your mindset to see payroll as part of a broader strategy for growth and efficiency, you can ensure it works for you, rather than simply being a cost.

Transforming employees from liabilities to assets requires effective management, focused development and engagement. It's about maximising potential, aligning skills with business objectives and ensuring they're contributing to overall success. Here are some strategies for achieving this transformation:

Set Clear Expectations and Provide Feedback:

- **Set Clear Goals:** Define specific, achievable performance targets for each employee.
- **Regular Feedback:** Offer constructive feedback regularly, recognising achievements and addressing areas for improvement.

Invest in Training and Development:

- **Skills Enhancement:** Identify gaps and provide relevant training to help employees develop essential skills.
- **Continuous Learning:** Promote ongoing learning through one-on-one training, online courses and development opportunities.

Improve Employee Engagement:

- **Involvement in Decision-making:** Involve employees in decisions to make them feel valued and connected to business success.
- **Recognition and Rewards:** Implement schemes to recognise contributions and celebrate achievements.

Create a Positive Work Environment:

- **Healthy Culture:** Encourage an inclusive and supportive workplace that values collaboration and respect.

- **Work-life Balance:** Offer flexible working arrangements and wellness programmes to support balance.

Provide Career Growth Opportunities:

- **Career Progression:** Help employees understand potential career paths and provide advancement opportunities.
- **Mentorship:** Establish mentorships to guide professional growth.

Address Performance Issues Promptly:

- **Improvement Plans:** Create clear performance improvement plans with objectives and timelines.
- **Support and Resources:** Ensure employees have the resources needed to meet expectations.

Enhance Communication:

- **Open Channels:** Maintain open communication between management and employees to address concerns and provide feedback.
- **Regular Check-ins:** Conduct one-on-one meetings to discuss progress and opportunities for improvement.

Leverage Strengths and Talents:

- **Strength-based Assignments:** Assign tasks that align with employees' strengths to maximise engagement.
- **Diverse Roles:** Offer role rotation to keep employees engaged, develop new skills and gain fresh perspectives.

Implement Effective Onboarding:

- **Comprehensive Onboarding:** Ensure new hires understand their roles, your business culture and expectations.
- **Buddy System:** Pair them with experienced colleagues to support integration and knowledge sharing.

Monitor and Measure Progress:

- **Performance Metrics:** Track employee progress using KPIs and adjust strategies as needed.
- **Regular Reviews:** Conduct performance reviews to provide guidance and assess development.

Offer Incentives and Motivation:

- **Incentives:** Introduce performance-based incentives to reward exceptional work.
- **Motivation:** A motivated workforce is productive; recognition schemes can drive this motivation.

Encourage Innovation and Ownership:

- **Responsibility:** Give employees ownership over their work, encouraging initiative and decision-making.
- **Innovation:** Encourage employees to suggest improvements, tapping into their potential to drive success.

Enhance Collaboration and Teamwork:

- **Collaboration:** Encourage teamwork and cross-departmental projects to integrate employees into the business.

- **Teamwork:** When employees work together effectively, they drive greater success than they could alone.

By applying these strategies, businesses can turn employees from liabilities into valuable assets that contribute positively to growth. The key is aligning personal growth with business goals, creating a positive environment and ensuring employees are supported in the right roles to make meaningful contributions. You need to offer employees enough challenge to inspire growth and development within their roles, while providing the support they need to feel confident in taking risks and stepping out of their comfort zones.

Grow Your Garden

I've mentioned different aspects of liabilities and assets for employees and payroll. Let me illustrate this with an analogy, to help explain their impact on your business.

Think of payroll management like managing a garden. If you invest in quality seeds, fertile soil and regular care, your garden will flourish and yield abundant, high-quality produce, which you can sell at higher prices. Similarly, a well-managed payroll, with competitive salaries and benefits, and a flexible working environment, nurtures skilled and motivated employees, turning them into valuable assets that drive higher business performance and revenue.

Conversely, if you skimp on garden care, using poor-quality seeds and neglecting maintenance, your yield will be sparse and of low quality, fetching lower prices. Similarly, neglecting your payroll management, offering low wages and poor benefits, and poor practice resulting in errors, confusion and misunderstandings, can result in unmotivated, unproductive employees, turning them into liabilities that drag down your business performance and profitability.

Basically, tend to your payroll (the garden) and your business will flourish. Bury your head in the sand and do the bare minimum, and your business will suffer the consequences.

Analysing your payroll in terms of liabilities and assets allows you to identify any issues; assessing how your payroll is functioning and supporting your business, and how it is holding your business back. Through this analysis, you'll be able to identify opportunities for improvement that can enhance the reputation of your business, its operational functionality and financial stability.

Main Points

- The return on investment into your employees and your payroll is in your hands; it's about how you view and manage them.

- Employees can be liabilities primarily due to costs, risks and potential negative impacts on your business' operations and reputation.

- Skilled and motivated employees drive productivity, innovation and success, while the payroll system ensures they're compensated accurately and on time, which builds trust and loyalty. Together, they form the heart of a thriving business, with employees contributing their time and talents, and payroll representing the business' commitment to its people.

- Changing payroll from a liability to an asset isn't something that can be done in a direct accounting sense, but you can certainly reframe the way payroll costs are managed and perceived within your business to drive more value.

- A well-managed payroll, with competitive salaries and benefits, and a flexible working environment, nurtures skilled and motivated employees, turning them into valuable assets that drive higher business performance and revenue.

Action Points

- **Liabilities and Assets:** List your employees and payroll as a liability, and how you can mitigate against those risks; and as an asset, detailing how you can maximise your investment.

CHAPTER 14

What's Your Business Worth?

Vision clear as day,
Payroll builds the firm's strong core,
Value grows with care.

Begin with the end in mind.

It's a well-worn phrase in business circles, but its importance can't be overstated. To steer your business in the right direction, you need to know exactly where you're heading. Once that's clear, you can work backwards, plotting the key milestones along the way and, crucially, translating them into actionable steps.

If you don't have a clear vision of your destination, you'll never arrive. Do you want your son or daughter to take over the business, or is your plan to sell up when you retire? Whatever your exit strategy, the goal is likely to be to build a business that can thrive without you. A worthy goal, even if you're staying at the helm, meaning your business works for you, not the other way around.

This means having robust internal processes, a sound pay structure and a team capable of keeping everything running smoothly in your absence. Without these, stepping away could risk bringing the entire operation down like a house of cards.

You need a solid vision of how your business will look, how it will function and what it will need to generate in revenue, without you there. This includes considering how your employee structure will evolve and what roles you'll require. You might not know the exact costs now - salaries will inevitably rise - but failing to plan for future pay expectations could be costly. The staffing and pay framework that works today won't be the same in 5, 10 or 15 years. Regular annual reviews are essential to keep your plans aligned with shifting realities.

Once you've nailed down a clear picture of your business' future, it's time to assess where you are now. Just as we covered in Chapter 12, there's power in understanding your current wage costs, expenses and staffing needs; it puts you firmly in control of your business. This forms your baseline. With that in hand, and a clear vision of where you're going, you can map the path to get there.

With payroll being your biggest expense, careful projection of what your business needs in terms of employee roles and pay is critical. We don't have a crystal ball and can't predict what government policy will do to tax rates and thresholds, NICs, statutory payments and the rest, but by analysing trends from the past three to five years, you can reasonably estimate future costs.

With thoughtful planning and sound financial management, you can build a business that serves you and your family well into the future. A business that not only lasts, but thrives.

In this chapter, I'll delve into the crucial elements of exit strategies and succession planning, focusing specifically on how payroll management can make or break a successful transition. I'll explore how payroll influences key aspects like business valuation, compliance and employee retention; factors that directly impact your business' attractiveness to potential buyers or successors. Whether you're planning to sell or pass your business on, ensuring payroll continuity, compliance and efficient processes will be critical for a smooth handover and maximising value. This chapter will guide you through the key payroll considerations that can safeguard your business' future and your team's trust.

Exit Strategy, Succession and Payroll

When planning an exit strategy, payroll is a crucial factor as it influences business valuation, attractiveness to buyers and the smoothness of the transition.

Here's how payroll impacts an effective exit plan:

Financial Health and Valuation: Efficient payroll management demonstrates strong cost control, which boosts the business' valuation. Buyers will closely examine payroll costs to assess profitability. Lower payroll expenses relative to revenue improve profit margins, making the business more appealing and potentially commanding a higher sale price.

Employee Retention and Stability: Retaining key employees is essential for a smooth transition. Offering competitive pay and retention bonuses helps keep staff on board during the handover, ensuring stability. Transparent payroll practices and fair treatment strengthen employee loyalty.

Due Diligence and Compliance: Accurate and transparent payroll records are key to making the due diligence process straightforward, helping to avoid hidden liabilities. Compliance with payroll regulations reduces legal risks and enhances the business' appeal to potential buyers.

Operational Efficiency: Streamlined payroll processes signal efficient operations; a positive indicator for buyers. Automating payroll reduces errors and saves time, presenting the business as well-managed.

Scalability and Growth Potential: Payroll systems that can scale with business growth are attractive to buyers, as they show room for expansion without a sharp rise in costs. Performance-based pay structures drive productivity and align employee goals with the business' growth, which can further increase buyer interest.

Employee Benefits and Compensation: A competitive compensation package helps attract and retain top talent, adding value to the business. While higher wages come with costs, these can be offset by increased revenue from a skilled and motivated workforce. Buyers are typically drawn to businesses with a well-compensated, efficient team.

Transition Planning: Clear communication with employees about the exit plan is vital to maintaining morale and productivity. Addressing potential changes to roles or pay early can help prevent disruption. Severance or redundancy packages should be factored into the exit plan if needed.

Reputation and Goodwill: Fair pay and benefits contribute to a positive work environment, which boosts the business' reputation and goodwill. A strong employer brand is attractive to buyers, especially those mindful of social responsibility.

Integrating payroll into your exit strategy ensures costs are managed, compliance is maintained and key employees are retained, all making the business more attractive to potential buyers. A strategic payroll approach can significantly impact the success of the sale and ensure a smooth transition to new ownership. However, this requires careful long-term planning and can't be rushed.

Even if you're passing the business to a family member, these considerations remain essential. A lean, well-structured payroll process will provide them with the best possible start, ensuring they inherit a solid, smooth-running business.

The key payroll elements to focus on for a smooth transition include:

Continuity and Knowledge Transfer: Ensure the new team understands the payroll system fully, with clear documentation of processes, including submissions, pension contributions and benefits.

Payroll Liabilities and Tax Obligations: Settle all outstanding payroll liabilities, ensuring tax obligations such as PAYE and pension contributions are up to date to avoid any legal or financial complications.

Pension and Benefits Administration: Ensure all contributions are current and responsibilities are clearly outlined for ongoing employee benefits.

Employee Contracts and TUPE Considerations: If applicable, ensure compliance with TUPE (Transfer of Undertakings [Protection of Employment]) regulations to preserve employee rights and avoid payroll interruptions.

Audit and Compliance: A payroll audit before exiting will help avoid any disputes, ensuring everything is in order from wage compliance to holiday pay.

Technology and System Updates: Make sure payroll systems remain functional post-handover. This may involve updating licences or ensuring a smooth transfer of employee data if the new owners have their own systems.

Exit Bonuses and Severance Pay: Any severance, redundancy or exit bonuses must be calculated correctly and in line with tax laws.

Payroll plays a vital role in exit or succession planning, helping ensure a smooth transition and protecting employee trust through effective communication. Careful attention to payroll continuity, compliance and record-keeping safeguards both the outgoing owner and the incoming team.

Future Planning

Employers need to carefully evaluate several aspects of payroll to ensure a smooth transition, compliance and financial stability when planning to exit the business.

Here are the key payroll-related factors that an employer should take into account:

Payroll Continuity and Succession Planning

Employers must ensure that payroll systems and processes continue smoothly during and after a leadership transition. This includes identifying key payroll personnel who will remain responsible for managing payroll during the transition period. If the person responsible for payroll is part of the succession plan or exit strategy, it's essential to train a successor to avoid disruptions in payroll management.

Considerations:

- Ensure that payroll knowledge is documented and shared with successors.
- Train staff or potential successors on payroll systems and processes to maintain continuity.
- Review third-party payroll providers, if in use, to ensure continued service through the transition.

Compliance with Legal and Tax Obligations

During exit strategies and succession planning, employers must continue to meet payroll-related legal and tax obligations such as PAYE, NICs and pension schemes. The risk of non-compliance may increase during transitions if details are overlooked, leading to potential fines and penalties.

Considerations:

- Ensure payroll taxes, NICs and pensions are calculated and submitted correctly, even during leadership changes.
- Conduct a compliance audit to ensure all obligations are being met.
- Ensure that changes in ownership or leadership don't impact payroll tax reporting and that any necessary changes to HMRC are communicated promptly.

Employee Contracts and Benefits

Payroll plays a crucial role in the financial stability of employees. Any changes during an exit or succession plan, such as restructuring or changes to contracts, can affect employees' pay, benefits or pensions. Employers must carefully manage payroll adjustments to protect employee morale and ensure legal compliance.

Considerations:

- Review employee contracts to ensure clarity on salaries, bonuses, benefits and other payroll-related entitlements.
- Consider any changes to payroll as part of the exit strategy, such as changes in pension schemes or bonuses.
- Ensure that any redundancy payments or severance packages are calculated and processed correctly through payroll.

Redundancies and Severance Payments

If the exit strategy includes downsizing or restructuring, redundancies may be necessary. This would impact payroll, as severance payments, holiday pay and any unpaid wages need to be calculated accurately. Failing to handle these properly can lead to legal disputes and negative employee sentiment.

Considerations:

- Ensure redundancy payments are calculated according to statutory guidelines and employee contracts.
- Accurately process final payslips, including holiday entitlements and outstanding wages.
- Manage the timing and communication of these payments to affected employees.
- Ensure strong, compassionate communication to employees throughout the process.

Pensions and Benefits Transfer

When there is a change in ownership or leadership, the responsibility for employee pensions and benefits needs careful attention. The new leadership must ensure that employee pension contributions continue without disruption and that any transfer of pension schemes is managed properly.

Considerations:

- Ensure pension schemes and contributions are maintained throughout the transition.
- Address how benefits such as health insurance, company cars or other non-monetary perks will be handled or transferred during the exit.

- Communicate with pension providers and employees about any changes to schemes or contributions.

Key Payroll Personnel

When planning for an exit or succession, it's essential to identify key personnel and consider how their roles might change. If they are part of the succession plan or are planning to exit, ensuring their payroll knowledge is passed on or documented is critical.

Considerations:
- Identify staff who may be involved in the succession planning process or have critical business knowledge that needs to be retained.
- If the key person is leaving, ensure a successor is trained and in place before the transition.
- Document processes and knowledge to prevent gaps in task management during leadership changes.

Shareholder and Director Remuneration

As part of an exit strategy, changes in the ownership structure may lead to adjustments in the remuneration of shareholders or directors. It is important to review how these payments are handled through payroll and whether there are any tax implications.

Considerations:
- Review how dividends, bonuses or salaries for directors or shareholders are managed within payroll.

- Ensure any changes in ownership are reflected in payroll systems and communicated to relevant parties, including HMRC.
- Consider tax planning around exit packages for departing directors or executives.

Payroll Due Diligence

For businesses being sold or going through a merger, payroll systems and records are subject to scrutiny during due diligence. Buyers will examine payroll to ensure accuracy, compliance and potential liabilities, such as outstanding tax obligations or unprocessed payments.

Considerations:
- Conduct a payroll audit to ensure compliance and accuracy before the due diligence process.
- Review payroll records for discrepancies, unpaid taxes or benefits liabilities that could affect the sale price or terms of the exit.
- Ensure that payroll systems are up to date, with accurate employee data, contracts and benefits information.

Succession and Pay Structure Adjustments

If a new leadership team or management structure is part of the succession plan, payroll systems may need to be adjusted to reflect changes in salaries, bonuses and compensation packages for new leadership roles.

Considerations:

- Update payroll systems to reflect any new pay structures for executives, managers or other key roles in the business.
- Address bonus structures or incentive schemes that may change with new leadership.
- Communicate these changes clearly to affected employees and ensure transparency in the payroll process.

Employee Engagement and Communication

During an exit or leadership transition, employees may feel uncertain about their future. Payroll is a sensitive area, as it directly impacts employees' livelihoods. Clear communication about any payroll-related changes, whether it's pay, benefits or pensions, is critical to maintain trust and engagement.

Considerations:

- Keep employees informed about any changes to payroll, benefits or pensions during the exit or succession process.
- Address concerns related to job security, pay continuity or bonus payments.
- Ensure employees have a point of contact within payroll for any payroll-related questions during the transition.

Employers considering exit strategies and succession planning must address payroll continuity, compliance, employee contracts and key personnel to ensure a smooth transition. Payroll plays a critical role in maintaining employee engagement and trust, while ensuring the business remains compliant with legal and financial obligations.

The Impact of Wage Structure on Business Saleability

The impact of wage structure on business saleability is critical because it directly influences how attractive your business is to potential buyers. A well-thought-out wage and benefits structure speaks to the financial health, operational efficiency and overall sustainability of the business, all of which are key factors when buyers are assessing whether a business is worth investing in.

If your wage structure is balanced and competitive, it shows that the business can manage costs effectively while retaining skilled employees. This keeps profit margins healthy and reduces turnover, which is appealing to buyers, because it means fewer disruptions and less money spent on recruitment or training. A stable, well-compensated workforce is a sign of operational stability. Buyers want to step into a business where key staff are in place and they don't have to worry about a mass exodus or rising wage bills.

Additionally, compliance with wage laws and employment regulations reduces the risk of future liabilities such as wage disputes or legal challenges. Buyers will look for businesses that are clean on compliance, as no one wants to inherit costly legal problems.

A wage structure that can scale with the business is also key. Buyers are interested in businesses with growth potential, and if the wage costs can grow without outpacing revenue, the business is far more appealing.

Finally, your wage structure can influence the reputation and goodwill of your business. Fair pay practices and competitive benefits help to build a positive working environment, which enhances your brand's reputation. A strong employer brand not only attracts talented employees, as discussed in Chapter 10, but also makes your business more appealing to buyers.

The wage structure isn't just about what you pay your staff; it's a reflection of your business' long-term viability, profitability and reputation. Buyers will assess it carefully to see how it impacts the future success of the business, which is why it's so important to get it right.

Manage Your Payroll to Boost Your Business' Sale Value

Maximising your business' sale value relies heavily on effective payroll management. As already mentioned, it plays a critical role in shaping your exit strategy and boosting overall business worth.

Here's how to maximise the impact of payroll on your sale value:

Optimise Workforce Costs: Regular payroll reviews ensure staffing is aligned with business needs, maintaining service quality without unnecessary expense. Automating payroll or outsourcing it can streamline operations and reduce internal costs.

Performance-based Incentives: Performance-based pay schemes like bonuses and commissions can drive productivity. A well-designed pay structure that rewards top performers enhances both talent retention and overall business performance.

Compliance and Risk Management: Staying on top of payroll regulations is essential to avoid legal risks. Regular audits, whether internal or external, help ensure financial records are accurate, minimising potential issues that could arise during a sale.

Employee Retention: Offering competitive wages and comprehensive benefits, such as health insurance or pensions, builds loyalty and reduces turnover. A stable, well-compensated workforce increases the attractiveness of your business to buyers.

Efficient Processes: Outsourcing payroll or integrating payroll systems with other business operations can reduce administrative burdens and ensure accuracy. Buyers appreciate businesses with efficient, well-organised processes.

Transparent Record-keeping: Maintaining clear, accurate payroll records is critical when preparing for a sale. Buyers will want reassurance that the business' finances are in order and that all payroll obligations are clearly documented.

Employee Development: Investing in staff training and cross-training not only improves productivity but also creates a more adaptable workforce, further increasing the value of your business.

Industry Benchmarking: Comparing your payroll practices against industry standards ensures you stay competitive and efficient, making your business more appealing to potential buyers.

Ultimately, your employees and your payroll are at the core of your business. Valuing your team and ensuring efficient payroll management strengthens your business' reputation, enhances productivity and makes your business more desirable to buyers.

Here are some things to consider:

Prepare Payroll for a Sale: Even if you're not planning to sell immediately, getting your payroll in order now will position your business for a smoother sale when the time comes.

Streamline Your Payroll System: Ensure your payroll processes are efficient, compliant and well-organised. Buyers will be drawn to businesses with seamless payroll operations. Invest in good payroll software or ensure that any outsourced payroll services meet required standards.

Ensure Compliance with Employment Laws: Your payroll process must comply with UK employment laws, from PAYE to minimum wage and pension contributions. Any non-compliance could deter buyers or lead to penalties during the sale process.

Audit Payroll and Employee Benefits: Carry out a full audit of payroll and benefits to ensure everything is up to date. Addressing any inconsistencies before entering negotiations can save time and prevent last-minute issues.

Document Payroll Procedures: Buyers want transparency and clarity. Create detailed documentation outlining payroll processes, tax submissions and employee benefits. This helps during the handover and reassures buyers of the business' efficiency.

Review Employee Contracts: Ensure all contracts reflect current benefits and legal obligations. Buyers will want clear information on any potential liabilities, so it's essential to have everything in order before negotiations.

Regular Financial Reviews: Payroll costs play a significant role in your business' financial health. Keep your financial statements up to date, with clear records of payroll expenses, to present a strong financial position to potential buyers.

Plan for Employee Liabilities: Address outstanding employee liabilities like unpaid bonuses or promised pay rises before the sale. This will prevent complications and make your business more attractive to buyers.

By taking these proactive steps to refine your payroll management, you will position your business for success, ultimately enhancing its attractiveness to potential buyers when the time comes to sell. Effective payroll management is more than just ensuring employees are paid on time; it plays a crucial role in the overall perception of your business' health and viability.

Know Your Business' Worth

Knowing the worth of your business and that its value is being optimised are crucial for employers, even if selling or succession isn't currently on the cards. Understanding the value of your business gives you clarity on where you stand, allows for better decision-making and keeps you prepared for any unexpected challenges or opportunities. It also helps identify areas that need improvement, be it financial efficiency, operational performance or employee satisfaction, all of which play a direct role in the long-term success and growth of your business.

Let's look at why knowing your business' value is important.

Strategic Decision-making: Knowing your business' worth allows you to make informed strategic decisions. Whether it's securing investment, taking on debt or planning an expansion, understanding your financial position helps you steer the business effectively. It also gives you a clearer picture of your payroll structure, helping you balance fair wages with business growth and profitability.

Preparedness for Unforeseen Circumstances: Life throws surprises, so having a clear understanding of your business' value ensures you're ready to act if circumstances change. Whether it's an unexpected offer to buy your business, the need to bring in new partners, or even planning for succession or retirement, knowing your worth ensures you won't be caught off guard.

Business Growth and Improvement: Valuing your business often highlights areas of strength and weakness. If your payroll system is inefficient or costing more than it should, a valuation process might flag this as an issue. Regularly reviewing your payroll and other financials ensures that your business is running as efficiently as possible, which in turn makes it more attractive to potential buyers or investors down the line.

Whether or not you plan to sell, knowing your business' value and ensuring that payroll is in order are smart moves for any employer. It not only keeps you informed and ready for the unexpected, but also helps to identify areas where you can enhance efficiency and profitability.

When the time does come for a sale or exit, having your payroll processes and procedures organised and compliant will significantly increase your business' appeal to potential buyers, ensuring a smoother transition with maximum value for you.

Main Points

- A well-planned payroll strategy can significantly impact the success of a sale and the smooth transition to new ownership.

- Employers considering exit strategies and succession planning must address payroll continuity, compliance, employee contracts and key personnel to ensure a smooth transition.

- A well-thought-out wage and benefits structure speaks to the financial health, operational efficiency and overall sustainability of the business, all of which are key factors when buyers are assessing whether a business is worth investing in.

- Even if a sale isn't on the immediate horizon, preparing your business now is a savvy move, and payroll is a key area to focus on.

- Effective payroll management is more than just ensuring employees are paid on time; it plays a crucial role in the overall perception of your business' health and viability.

Action Points

- **Exit Goal:** Set a timeline and vision for your business, like selling in 10 years. Assess your current payroll structure and costs, and estimate what they'll be at your exit.

- **Exit Readiness:** Identify areas to improve for boosting your business' sale value. Plan steps to ensure the right structure and finances are in place, maximising payroll's contribution to your business' value.

CHAPTER 15

The Value of Payroll to Profit

Payroll's careful eye,
Shaping profits, keeping flow,
Balance fuels the growth.

Profit is the lifeblood of your business. Without profit, a business stalls. It's what fuels growth, drives innovation and keeps the wheels turning. Many businesses focus on increasing revenue as the key to boosting profit, and payroll plays a critical role in this.

In this chapter, we'll explore the intricate relationship between payroll and profit, and how payroll can support with profit generation and stability. As mentioned earlier, payroll is often seen as a cost to be managed. Payroll can either support or undermine profit generation, depending on how it's handled. From optimising workforce costs to motivating staff through well-structured pay, payroll has a direct impact on the profitability of a business. We'll look at how a strategically managed payroll can help drive profit, control costs and ensure that your business engine runs smoothly.

What's Important About Profit?

Profit is critical because it's what keeps your business running, fuels growth and ensures long-term stability. Without profit, you can't reinvest, reward employees or expand, and of course pay yourself. It's more than just a number; it's the foundation that allows a business to thrive. When it comes to payroll, understanding how it impacts profit is vital for any employer aiming to manage costs and maximise revenue.

Why Profit Matters

Sustainability and Survival: Profit ensures your business can continue to operate, meet its financial obligations and weather downturns. It's what allows you to keep the doors open and pay your staff on time. But if payroll costs aren't controlled, they can quickly eat into profits, making sustainability harder to maintain.

Fuel for Growth: Profit is what enables your business to grow, whether that's by investing in new technologies, hiring more staff or expanding into new markets. For you as an employer, it's a delicate balance; you need to ensure your payroll costs support your business' growth rather than hinder it. Hiring strategically or investing in staff training can drive productivity and contribute to long-term profit.

Cash Flow and Stability: Profit keeps cash flow healthy, which is crucial for paying bills, covering payroll and dealing with unexpected expenses. If payroll costs are mismanaged, even a profitable business can struggle with cash flow. It's essential to ensure payroll spending aligns with revenue so there's always enough cash to cover employee wages, without straining your business' finances.

Employee Retention and Motivation: A profitable business can reward employees properly, which in turn helps retain top talent and boost productivity. But the key is managing payroll so that wages and benefits are competitive, without overstretching the budget. Profit enables employers to invest in their workforce but payroll has to be structured in a way that supports profit, rather than drains it.

Payroll Can Support Profit Generation: Payroll isn't just a cost centre. When managed properly, it can contribute to profit generation.

Here's how:

Optimising Labour Costs: By carefully managing payroll, you can ensure you're getting the most value from your workforce. This means aligning staffing levels with business demand, avoiding overstaffing that inflates payroll costs or understaffing that leads to burnout and inefficiency. Using payroll data to track patterns, like overtime or productivity, can highlight areas where adjustments can improve profitability.

Boosting Productivity: Payroll plays a key role in employee motivation. Paying staff fairly and on time, offering competitive benefits and rewarding hard work through bonuses or performance-based pay all help boost morale and productivity. A more motivated, engaged workforce is more efficient, which directly supports profit generation.

Managing Compliance and Avoiding Costs: Outsourced payroll services, or a well-trained internal payroll team, ensure that your business stays compliant with tax laws, NICs, pensions and other regulations. Getting this wrong can lead to hefty fines or penalties, which eat into profits. An efficient payroll system helps avoid these risks, keeping your business running smoothly and your profit intact.

Controlling Overtime and Variable Pay: You need to keep an eye on overtime costs, as these can quickly spiral out of control and erode profits. Payroll can help by tracking hours worked and identifying where overtime is costing the business too much. In some cases, it might be more profitable to hire additional staff rather than relying on regular overtime. Having this data allows you to make informed decisions that protect profitability.

Workforce Planning and Flexibility: A well-structured payroll system provides valuable data that can inform workforce planning. For example, seasonal businesses can use payroll insights to scale up or down according to demand, avoiding unnecessary payroll expenses during quieter periods. Flexibility in payroll, such as using part-time staff or temporary workers, can help businesses manage costs more efficiently, ensuring payroll supports rather than undermines profit.

Data-driven Decisions: Modern payroll systems provide detailed reports on workforce costs, productivity and employee performance. This data helps you make informed decisions about staffing levels, pay structures and resource allocation. By analysing this data, you can spot inefficiencies, manage costs better and find ways to maximise the profitability of your workforce.

Profit is essential for growth, stability and success. Payroll, being probably the largest expense, has a direct impact on profit. However, when managed well, payroll can support profit generation, rather than just being a cost. By using payroll strategically, optimising workforce costs, boosting productivity, ensuring compliance and leveraging data for smarter decisions, you can ensure that payroll plays a key role in protecting and driving your business' profitability.

The Value Payroll Can Provide for Your Profit

Payroll offers a range of critical benefits which directly support profit generation. Streamlining payroll management can let you focus on your core operations, rather than getting bogged down in admin tasks.

Below shows how a good payroll process can contribute to a business' bottom line.

Efficiency and Time-saving: Managing payroll is complex and time-consuming for large workforce businesses or those with complicated pay structures, or for small businesses, where you're in charge of this important task. Outsourcing payroll to a specialist saves time that can be reinvested into more profit-generating areas, allowing key personnel to focus on driving revenue.

Cost Control and Reduction: By analysing payroll data you can identify cost-saving opportunities such as reducing unnecessary overtime or optimising benefit offerings. This helps to control workforce costs – a critical component for the overall profitability of your business.

Cost Efficiency: Outsourcing payroll can save money in the long run. This is because payroll bureaux use specialised software and are experts in navigating payroll tax, compliance and regulation updates efficiently. Lower operational costs directly help boost profit margins. Outsourcing reduces the need for in-house resources to manage payroll, eliminates costly mistakes and provides scalability as your business grows. You avoid potential penalties from compliance issues, making it a cost-effective solution.

Compliance and Risk Management: Payroll ensures that businesses remain compliant with ever-changing UK employment laws, tax regulations and pension contributions, reducing the risk of costly penalties or fines. Avoiding these financial pitfalls protects a business' profitability and financial health.

Employee Satisfaction and Retention: Timely and accurate payroll ensures employees are paid correctly, which helps maintain morale and trust. Happy, well-compensated employees are more productive and less likely to leave, which reduces costly turnover and the expenses of recruiting and training new staff.

Data-driven Insights: Payroll generates a lot of data. This can be valuable for making informed business decisions. By analysing payroll data, you can identify trends in areas such as workforce costs, absenteeism and overtime patterns. This gives you a clearer picture of workforce productivity and where resources are being spent. It's actionable information that can help with budgeting, planning and improving efficiency.

Financial Reporting, Planning and Budgeting: Payroll software provides detailed reports and insights that can be used for strategic planning. Accurate data on employee costs, overtime, bonuses and other payroll metrics can help you make informed decisions about workforce investments, budget allocations and areas to cut costs, all of which influence profitability. Accurate payroll data is essential for financial planning and budgeting. It helps project future costs, managing cash flow and making strategic decisions about hiring, pay rises and bonuses.

Scalability: As your business grows, your payroll needs become more complex. Outsourced payroll can scale up efficiently to meet these demands without requiring additional in-house resources. This flexibility ensures that the business can maintain its focus on growth and profit generation without worrying about payroll headaches.

By optimising these areas, payroll can free up resources, reduce risk and enhance the overall financial performance of the business, making payroll a valuable contributor to an employer's profit generation strategy.

Understanding Your Profit in Payroll Terms

You can better understand your profit by looking at how payroll costs impact your overall business performance and profitability.

Below are some key points to consider.

Labour Costs as a Percentage of Revenue: A simple way to assess the relationship between payroll and profit is to calculate how much of your business' revenue goes towards paying wages, salaries and benefits. If payroll costs are too high in relation to revenue, profits will suffer. You should regularly review this percentage to ensure that your workforce costs are aligned with income.

Gross Profit per Employee: This is calculated by dividing the business' gross profit by the total number of employees. It shows how much profit each employee is generating for the business. If this figure is lower than expected, it might indicate inefficiencies in workforce utilisation or overstaffing.

Payroll as a Fixed and Variable Cost: You need to recognise which parts of payroll are fixed and which are variable. Salaries are generally fixed costs, whereas hourly pay, overtime or bonuses can fluctuate. Understanding this distinction helps businesses forecast better and identify areas where costs can be trimmed without compromising productivity.

Overtime Costs Impact on Profit: Excessive overtime can quickly erode profits. You should track overtime payments closely and assess whether it's more cost-effective to hire additional staff or restructure shifts to manage workloads more efficiently. Too much reliance on overtime can be a sign of understaffing, which in the long term could be more expensive than expanding the team.

Employee Turnover and Recruitment Costs: High employee turnover can heavily impact profit when factoring in the costs associated with recruiting, onboarding and training new staff. You should evaluate how well you are retaining talent, as a stable workforce leads to more predictable payroll costs and fewer disruptions to productivity, both of which protect profit margins.

Productivity and Payroll Ratios: You should consider productivity in relation to payroll. If payroll costs are rising but productivity isn't improving, profits will inevitably shrink. Businesses can measure productivity through output-per-hour metrics or other KPIs relevant to your industry. Ensuring that payroll spending is matched by output helps protect profitability.

Pension Contributions and Benefits: Beyond salaries, you need to factor in the costs of pensions, NICs and other employee benefits. These are vital for compliance and employee satisfaction, but they still need to be managed efficiently to avoid eating too far into profits. Regularly reviewing benefits packages can ensure they remain competitive without becoming a financial drain.

You need to monitor and manage payroll as a critical business expense that directly impacts profitability. By understanding these metrics, you can make informed decisions on hiring, pay structures and overall workforce management, ensuring that payroll supports profit generation, rather than hindering it.

Payroll is known as an expense – a cost to the business – and it is, but through payroll's support and efficient management it can provide great value and assist with increasing profit within your business.

The Evolution of Profit Management in Relation to Payroll

The evolution of profit management and cost control has been shaped by advances in technology, changing employment practices and increasing regulation. Over time, employers are refining their payroll processes, focusing more on maximising profitability while keeping workforce costs in check.

Below, I look at this evolution in more detail.

Manual Processes to Automation

Historically, payroll management was a manual process, often involving paper timesheets, hand-calculated wages and manual tax deductions. This was labour-intensive, error-prone and time-consuming, making cost control difficult. Mistakes in payroll could lead to overpayments, tax issues and compliance problems, all of which could cut into profits.

As payroll software emerged, processes became more automated. Due to this, and being supported by the development and strengthening of payroll processes and procedures, employers were able to reduce errors, improve efficiency and gain greater control over their payroll costs. Automation made it easier to track payroll expenses in real time, offering clearer insights into how labour costs were impacting the bottom line.

Basic Payroll Management to Strategic Workforce Planning

In the early days, payroll was simply about getting employees paid correctly and on time. But as businesses became more focused on profitability, the role of payroll evolved. Employers started using payroll data to make strategic decisions about their workforce, such as optimising staff levels, reviewing pay structures and forecasting workforce costs. This analytical resource generated by payroll software and processes has barely been touched on by employers, and has much more to give.

This shift means that payroll is no longer just an operational function; it has become a tool for driving profitability. Employers should look at metrics like revenue per employee, workforce costs as a percentage of turnover, and other KPIs to control costs and increase profit margins.

Cost-cutting to Value Maximisation

Previously, payroll cost control was largely about cutting expenses where possible, reducing staff, freezing wages or cutting benefits to boost short-term profits. However, businesses are realising that simply slashing payroll costs could lead to negative outcomes, like reduced productivity, low employee morale and high turnover, all of which harm profits in the long run.

Today, the approach should be more about value maximisation. Instead of cutting costs blindly, you should ensure that your payroll investment delivers the most value for your business. This could mean investing in training to increase employee productivity, offering competitive salaries to retain top talent or optimising shift patterns to get the most out of the workforce, without incurring excessive overtime costs.

Compliance-driven to Technology-enhanced

The need for compliance, especially with UK regulations around NICs, pensions, NMW and tax, has always been a key driver in payroll management. In the past, businesses had to allocate significant resources to ensure compliance, as mistakes could result in hefty fines that erode profits.

With continual modernisation of payroll systems and integration of payroll processes and procedures throughout the business, it has become far more streamlined. Modern systems handle tax calculations, pension contributions and compliance updates, freeing up payroll to focus on more strategic tasks that bring value to the business. This not only ensures compliance, but reduces administrative costs and enhances profitability.

Workforce Flexibility

The rise in the number of temporary workers and more flexible working arrangements have changed how employers manage payroll. The traditional model of full-time, permanent staff has given way to a mix including part-time, fixed-term, and ad hoc workers. This shift has given employers more control over payroll costs, allowing them to scale workforce expenses up or down, depending on business demand.

While this flexibility has provided opportunities for cost control, it has also added complexity to payroll management. Employers must now track various pay rates, contract terms and tax obligations, making modern payroll systems essential for managing these costs effectively.

Data-driven Decision-making

In recent years, data analytics has transformed payroll management. Employers can now analyse payroll data to spot trends, identify inefficiencies and make informed decisions about their workforce. For example, analytics can reveal patterns of absenteeism or excessive overtime, helping businesses make adjustments that reduce costs and improve productivity.

Data-driven insights allow businesses to optimise payroll spending, ensuring that every pound invested in wages and benefits contributes to profit generation. This represents a significant shift from the past, where payroll management was more reactive and less informed by real-time data.

Integration with Broader Business Strategy

Today, payroll isn't just a back-office function, nor is it a 'push button' task; it needs to be integrated into the broader business strategy. You need to recognise that your workforce is one of your biggest assets and how you manage payroll has a direct impact on profitability. By aligning payroll with long-term business goals such as growth or expansion, you can ensure that your payroll practices support, rather than hinder, profit generation.

The evolution of profit management and cost control, when considering payroll, has moved from basic, manual processes to a more strategic, technology-driven and data-analysing approach. You should view payroll as a key driver of profitability, using data, technology and modern workforce practices to manage costs more effectively and maximise the value of your investment in your people.

A Strategic Tool in Profit Management

Payroll is far more than just an administrative task. When used properly, it's a powerful strategic tool in profit management, cost control and budgeting. Employers who view payroll through this lens can make smarter decisions about their workforce, align costs with business goals and, ultimately, drive profitability.

Payroll plays a central role in managing profit because, as mentioned, the workforce is one of your biggest expenses. By managing payroll strategically, you can directly influence profitability.

Here are some ways you can make this happen:

Maximising Employee Value: Payroll isn't just a cost; it's an investment in your people. When structured effectively, it ensures that every pound spent on wages, benefits and bonuses delivers value back to the business through productivity, innovation and employee retention. The key is making sure that what's paid out matches what's coming back in terms of contribution to the business' growth and success.

Driving Revenue: By strategically investing in payroll, whether that's through performance-based pay, training or hiring key talent, employers can drive higher revenue. Productive, well-compensated staff are motivated to perform at their best, directly contributing to profit generation.

A Tool for Cost Control: Payroll can also be a crucial tool for controlling costs, helping you manage your budget more effectively and allowing you to protect your profit margins.

Workforce Cost Management: Payroll allows employers to track and manage workforce costs in real time. By monitoring trends in wages, overtime and employee turnover, you can identify areas where costs are creeping up and take steps to address them. For example, if overtime is consistently high, it might indicate understaffing or underperformance. Hiring additional workers or investing in training could save money in the long run.

Flexibility in Workforce Planning: Payroll data can provide insights into whether your current staffing model is working. Is the business overstaffed in quiet periods? Are you relying too much on temporary staff, and fluctuating between being overstaffed and understaffed? By using payroll strategically, employers can create a more flexible workforce model that adjusts to business needs, keeping workforce costs in check without sacrificing productivity.

Avoiding Costly Compliance Errors: Payroll service providers and well-trained internal payroll staff ensure compliance with tax laws, pension regulations, NICs, employment law and all the rest. Getting this wrong can lead to costly fines and penalties. By ensuring payroll is compliant and up to date, businesses avoid these risks, keeping costs under control and protecting their profit.

Payroll in Budgeting and Financial Planning: Payroll also plays a pivotal role in budgeting and financial planning. Accurate payroll data helps employers forecast workforce costs, plan for growth and ensure they are making informed financial decisions.

Forecasting Payroll Costs: Payroll is, for the best part, a predictable expense, but it's one that needs to be carefully forecasted. You can use payroll data to anticipate future costs, such as wage increases, new hires or changes in NICs or pension contributions, allowing you to plan ahead and allocate resources effectively, preventing overrun and eating into profits.

Aligning Payroll with Business Objectives: Effective budgeting isn't just about cutting costs; it's about aligning spending with business goals. By planning payroll strategically you can ensure that you are investing in the right areas, whether that's hiring key roles, offering performance incentives or upskilling current staff. This ensures that payroll supports your business' long-term goals and growth strategy, rather than becoming a financial burden.

Contingency Planning: Payroll data can also support contingency planning. If your business hits a rough patch, having a clear understanding of workforce costs helps you make informed decisions about where to make adjustments, without causing too much disruption to the workforce or overall business operations.

Payroll, when viewed strategically, is a powerful tool for profit management, cost control and budgeting. It's not just about paying staff, but about ensuring that payroll aligns with your business' financial goals, supports growth and helps manage costs effectively. By using payroll data to inform decisions, employers can ensure their workforce is an asset to profitability, not a drain. Strategic payroll management means smarter spending, better productivity and, ultimately, a healthier bottom line.

Examples of How Payroll Supports You and Your Profit

Obtaining External Funding:

Challenge: A community-based employer was required to apply for funding to hire an employee for a specific project.
Solution: The employer sought the knowledge and experience of a payroll professional to build a data-driven and practical estimate of the costs of hiring and paying the employee over the length of the project. The payroll professional provided the employer with a comprehensive cost analysis to present in their funding application.
Outcome: The cost analysis, backed up with real-life data, was accepted by the funding providers, and the funding was granted.

Permission to Proceed from a Board of Directors:

Challenge: A charity employer was required to present costs of a pay rise for existing employees to the board of directors for approval, before they could raise employees' pay.
Solution: Using payroll knowledge and experience, and payroll data, estimated pay projections for employees could be provided, based on different scenarios, to estimate the cost to the charity of raising employees' pay.
Outcome: Presented with solid, estimated pay projections, supported and grounded by data and a number of options, the board of directors could make an informed decision on the pay rises, allowing employees to receive more pay whilst managing cost implications for the charity.

Optimising Overtime Costs in Manufacturing:

Challenge: A mid-sized UK manufacturing business was struggling with high overtime costs, which were eating into its profit margins. Despite steady revenue, the business was finding that a significant portion of its profits were being swallowed up by overtime payments, as they regularly required staff to work extra hours to meet production deadlines.
Solution: By analysing payroll data, the business identified that overtime spikes were occurring in predictable patterns, often during the same times each month. Using this data, the business decided to restructure its workforce, bringing in part-time staff during peak periods rather than relying heavily on overtime.
Outcome: This change dramatically reduced overtime costs. Although bringing in part-time workers created a slightly higher payroll during peak periods, the overall savings from reduced overtime were substantial. Profit margins improved and the business found that employees were less fatigued and more productive without the excessive overtime hours. Payroll management directly supported more efficient cost control and boosted profitability by reallocating

workforce resources where they were needed most, and boosted employee morale and performance.

Boosting Profitability through Strategic Hiring in Hospitality:

Challenge: A small but growing UK-based hospitality chain was struggling to keep up with the demand for its services, particularly during busy seasons. It faced high employee turnover, which led to excessive spending on recruitment and training. As a result, it was spending heavily on payroll without seeing a significant return in terms of productivity or profit growth.
Solution: The business used payroll data to identify trends in staffing costs and turnover rates. It became clear that temporary staff were costing more than they were worth due to frequent retraining and reduced efficiency. Instead of continuing this cycle, the business decided to invest in full-time, permanent staff who could be trained properly and offer better long-term value.
Outcome: By restructuring its hiring approach, the business reduced its payroll costs in terms of recruitment and training, and saw an increase in employee productivity and retention. Full-time staff, with a more stable payroll, were more engaged, provided better service to the business' clients and contributed to the overall growth of the business. Payroll management allowed the business to make data-driven decisions that reduced long-term costs and supported stronger profit generation.

Payroll Compliance and Profit Protection in Retail:

Challenge: A small UK retail business faced issues with payroll compliance. It was managing payroll in-house, but frequently missing important regulatory changes, particularly around NICs and auto-enrolment pensions. As a result, the business incurred several penalties that hurt its bottom line.

Solution: The business decided to outsource payroll to a specialist provider who ensured that the business stayed up to date with all relevant legislation and compliance requirements. This outsourced payroll service took over the handling of tax deductions, pensions and NICs reducing the risk of future penalties, and freed up internal resources.

Outcome: By using a payroll service to manage compliance, the business avoided future fines, which significantly improved its financial stability. It also gained peace of mind knowing that the payroll was handled accurately, allowing management to focus on growing the business rather than worrying about compliance issues. The outsourcing of payroll also led to more predictable workforce costs, which helped in budgeting and profit forecasting.

Using Payroll Data for Financial Forecasting in Tech:

Challenge: A fast-growing UK tech startup was expanding its workforce rapidly, but the founders were unsure how much to budget for future hires. It needed a clearer picture of how payroll costs would scale alongside revenue growth, as its financial forecasting was largely speculative.

Solution: The business turned to payroll for insights. It used payroll data to track current staff costs, including salaries, benefits and taxes, and projected these costs over the next few years based on expected headcount increases. By factoring in potential salary increases, bonuses and benefit contributions, the business was able to build a more accurate financial forecast.

Outcome: With a clearer understanding of how payroll would evolve, the business could better manage its cash flow and budget for expansion. It avoided over-hiring early on, which helped protect profit margins, while still ensuring it had the right talent in place to support growth. Payroll data gave the business the visibility it needed to align staffing costs with its financial goals and growth plans. This allowed it to scale its operations in a sustainable way, which ensured continuity of the business.

Reducing Turnover through Data-driven Insights:

Challenge: An online retailer was faced with high employee turnover in its fulfilment centres, which were costly and disruptive.
Solution: The employer analysed payroll and attendance data to identify patterns of absenteeism and turnover. By cross-referencing payroll data with work schedules and performance metrics, it discovered specific periods and shifts when turnover spiked, and shift times with high stress.
Outcome: By using payroll data, the employer adjusted shift scheduling, implemented targeted retention bonuses, provided the right support where it was needed most, and improved communication about pay and benefits. This led to a reduction in turnover rates and improved employee satisfaction.

These case studies illustrate payroll management as a strategic tool for improving financial outcomes. Whether through cost control or more accurate budgeting, these businesses were able to use payroll data and processes to directly support profit generation and long-term financial stability. You could do the same!

Payroll, Profit and You

When it comes to payroll, profit and you, there's a delicate balancing act at play. On one hand, payroll is most often the largest expense for a business. On the other hand, it's a key driver of productivity and growth. The interaction between payroll and profit needs to be carefully managed to ensure financial stability, while keeping employees happy and motivated.

Payroll as a Profit Driver

You need to recognise that payroll isn't just an expense; it's an investment. The right payroll structure can directly contribute to profit by ensuring your staff are productive, motivated and aligned with the business' goals.

Here are three key areas for investment:

Employee Motivation and Productivity: Paying competitive wages and offering performance-based incentives can boost employee morale and productivity. A well-paid, engaged workforce is more likely to go the extra mile, deliver higher-quality work and contribute to the bottom line. Payroll acts as a tool to drive profitability by rewarding performance that fuels business success.

Attracting and Retaining Talent: In a competitive market, the ability to attract and retain top talent is crucial. If payroll is managed strategically, it ensures that businesses can offer the right salaries and benefits to keep skilled workers on board. The cost of high employee turnover, recruitment, training and lost productivity can far outweigh the expense of a well-structured payroll system. Employers who get this balance right, protect their profit margins by reducing these hidden costs.

Scaling for Growth: As a business grows, so do its payroll needs. However, using payroll strategically, you can ensure that your workforce scales in line with revenue growth. For example, bringing in part-time or flexible staff during peak times can keep payroll in line with demand, supporting profit generation without unnecessary cost inflation.

Payroll's Impact on Profit

Despite these benefits, in reality, payroll can quickly become a financial burden if not managed properly. For many businesses, especially smaller ones, payroll costs can easily spiral out of control and wage bills can seriously eat into profit margins. This leaves little left for investment or for paying yourself.

Below are three key areas to keep tight control of:

Bloated Payroll Costs: One of the key risks is overstaffing or offering salaries that are unsustainable for the business' revenue level. When payroll costs balloon, it can choke off profit, leaving the business struggling to reinvest or even meet its basic financial obligations. If you don't keep a tight rein on payroll, you can find yourself in a situation where the business is barely breaking even, despite healthy revenue.

Overtime and Variable Pay: Overtime can be a sneaky drain on profitability. While it might seem like a good short-term solution to ramp up productivity, regular overtime can quickly add up, pushing payroll costs higher than expected. If you fail to manage these additional payments your profits will erode, especially if there isn't a corresponding increase in output or revenue.

Compliance and Payroll Penalties: Failing to stay on top of payroll compliance, whether it's PAYE, NICs, pensions or other regulations, can lead to hefty fines and penalties. Not only does this impact profit directly, but it also damages cash flow, creates unnecessary administrative burdens and can hurt the business' reputation.

Financial Management and Control

Effective payroll management is critical to maintain control over your business' finances. When you have a solid grasp on payroll you can more easily manage cash flow, budget accurately, and avoid nasty surprises that could harm profitability.

Here's why:

Cash-flow Management: Payroll is a non-negotiable expense and managing it well is key to ensuring consistent cash flow. If payroll costs outstrip revenue, even temporarily, it can lead to a cash-flow crisis that impacts the day-to-day running of your business. You need to ensure that your payroll commitments match your revenue cycles, allowing for flexibility where necessary.

Budgeting and Forecasting: Payroll data is a powerful tool for forecasting workforce costs and planning for future growth. Employers who integrate payroll into their financial planning can budget more effectively, ensuring that payroll costs are aligned with business objectives and profitability targets. This kind of forward planning allows you to anticipate future payroll expenses, such as wage increases or additional hires, and avoid nasty shocks that could derail financial stability.

A Tool for Profit Protection

Payroll can be used in such a way to protect profit, especially when businesses face financial challenges.

Here are two ways you can do this:

Flexible Workforce Models: In times of economic uncertainty or seasonal fluctuations, having a flexible payroll model, such as using part-time staff or ad hoc workers, can help keep workforce costs under control. This flexibility allows businesses to scale back during quieter periods without the financial burden of full-time staff. Payroll, in this sense, becomes a tool for controlling costs and safeguarding profit during leaner times. Bear in mind that your employees' working patterns will determine the correct type of contract. If they are working regular hours, then a salary or fixed-hour contract is appropriate. If they are purely ad hoc working, with hours going up and down, and weeks where no hours are worked, then an ad hoc (zero-hour) contract might be appropriate. At the time of writing, ad hoc worker contracts are being reviewed, with legislation and guidance on use of these types of contract being tightened.

Data-driven Decisions: Payroll data can offer valuable insights into workforce costs, productivity and efficiency. If you use this data strategically, you can make informed decisions about where to cut costs, how to allocate resources and when to invest in your workforce. By using payroll as a source of business intelligence, you can protect your profit while maintaining operational efficiency.

The relationship between payroll and profit is one of balance. Payroll can be a major financial burden or a key driver of business growth. You need to manage this dynamic carefully, using payroll as a strategic tool to support profit generation, while keeping costs in check. The key is to view payroll not just as an unavoidable expense, but as an integral part of your business' financial management and cost control strategy.

When payroll is aligned with your business goals, managed effectively and used strategically, it becomes a powerful lever for enhancing profitability. But, when left unchecked, it can quickly undermine the financial health of your business. The real challenge lies in striking the right balance. Get this right, and you'll have a lean, profitable business that's more appealing to buyers, ready to be passed on to the next generation, and far more enjoyable for you to run.

Main Points

- Payroll can free up resources, reduce risk and enhance the overall financial performance of the business, making it a valuable contributor to an employer's profit generation strategy.
- You need to monitor and manage payroll as a critical business expense that directly impacts profitability. By understanding the metrics, you can make informed decisions on hiring, pay structures and overall workforce management, ensuring that payroll supports profit generation, rather than hindering it.
- Today, the approach should be more about value maximisation. Instead of cutting costs blindly, you should look to ensure that your payroll investment delivers the most value for the business.
- By using payroll strategically, optimising workforce costs, boosting productivity, ensuring compliance and leveraging data for smarter decisions, you can ensure that it plays a key role in protecting and driving your business' profitability.
- Strategic payroll management means smarter spending, better productivity and, ultimately, a healthier bottom line.

Action Points

- **Payroll Profit Strategy:** Identify key profit areas in your business and adjust your payroll structure to support better margins.
- **KPIs:** Set payroll KPIs to cut costs and increase profits. Track metrics like labour costs as a percentage of revenue, gross profit per employee, fixed and variable payroll costs, overtime, turnover, recruitment costs and productivity ratios, and seek improvements.

CHAPTER 16

Summary

Process builds the base,
People first, profits in place,
Payroll keeps the pace.

This book has touched on various aspects of paying your employees and, I hope, given you an insightful look into the complexities and importance of payroll. Payroll is often seen as just a large expense in a business, but I hope that after reading this book you now recognise the immense value it holds beyond being a cost. There's much more to payroll than meets the eye. If it is embraced fully, I believe payroll can transform your business in ways you never expected.

At the heart of this transformation lie the 3 Ps of Payroll: Process, People and Profit.

Process

Payroll is a vital business process, but it's often underestimated. It's more than just pushing a button to pay your employees. Payroll management touches every aspect of your operations, from maintaining compliance with complex regulations to ensuring timely, accurate payments that keep your employees satisfied. An efficient payroll process reduces risks, mitigates errors and increases operational efficiency. By investing in your payroll process you're investing in smoother, more streamlined business operations.

People

People are the driving force behind every successful business, and payroll is the linchpin that connects you with your team. A well-managed payroll process creates trust, loyalty and satisfaction among employees. When people are paid correctly and on time, it speaks volumes about how much you value them. It's not just about the financial reward; it's about the message that your business cares for its people, recognises their efforts and ensures their well-being. Investing in payroll is investing in your people and, ultimately, in your business culture and employee retention.

Profit

Profitability may seem disconnected from payroll at first glance, but nothing could be further from the truth. Payroll is a strategic business function that directly impacts the bottom line. From ensuring compliance with tax laws (thus avoiding costly penalties) to improving employee morale and productivity, payroll has the power to support business growth and profitability. Treating payroll as an investment means you're not only protecting your business from unnecessary risks, but driving it towards sustainable success.

Payroll is more than just a necessary task; it's the driving force behind many successful business initiatives, especially when it comes to your people. A well-managed payroll can transform workplace culture, creating a positive ripple effect that changes how your business is viewed, both from the inside and out.

Your payroll is tied to what your employees value most and is often your business' biggest cost. By investing in it, you can unlock the real value that a well-run payroll can bring.

As I've said, this book was never intended to be a 'how to' guide on processing payroll – that would have been a far bigger book and outdated before you even finished it. Instead, we've just scratched the surface of the technical details. The goal here was to help you see payroll from a fresh perspective. I love payroll, and I understand the countless ways it can positively impact a business. I see so many business owners missing out on its potential, simply because they don't see payroll for what it could be.

You have the opportunity to turn what might feel like your biggest headache into one of your greatest business assets. Don't let your payroll control you; make it work for you.

Hayley

What Now?

I understand I've provided you with a lot of information throughout this book, and you might be wondering, *where on earth do I begin?* The key is not to feel overwhelmed. Every business is unique. You can work through the action points at the end of each chapter, focusing on what's most relevant and pressing for your particular business.

To help you gain some initial clarity and momentum, I've outlined three simple steps to get you started on your payroll journey:

1. **Assess Your Current Payroll Process**
   Before you can determine where you want to go, you need a clear understanding of where you are now. Take a good, honest look at your payroll process as it stands today. What's working well, and where are the pain points? This isn't just about the financial cost, but also the time, effort and human cost of processing your payroll. Engage with your employees and everyone involved in the payroll cycle; their insights will be invaluable. Look at the resources it consumes, the systems in place and the overall impact it has on your business operations. This will give you a solid foundation on which to build.

2. **Define Your Ideal Payroll Process**
   Once you know where you are, the next step is to get clear on where you want to be. What does your ideal payroll process look like? Think about the improvements you'd like to see. Do you want to streamline operations to save time? Do you want to improve accuracy to reduce errors and compliance risks? Or perhaps increase transparency to boost employee trust and satisfaction? Paint a picture of what a perfect payroll process would look like for your business; one that aligns with your broader goals and values.

3. **Map Out the Steps for Improvement**
   Now that you have a clear understanding of your current process and a vision of where you want to be, it's time to map out the steps to bridge that gap. What changes can you implement to move towards your ideal payroll process? It could involve investing in better payroll software, refining your payroll policies or providing more training for your team. Each step you take should be aimed at maximising the value that payroll can bring to your business. Remember, payroll is not just a cost centre; it's a strategic function that can enhance your business' efficiency, employee satisfaction and, ultimately, its profitability.

These three steps are just the beginning. By regularly reviewing and refining your payroll processes, you'll ensure that your business continues to benefit from the value payroll can provide. The journey will take time and is never-ending, but with each improvement you'll see the positive impact it can have on your business, your people and your profits. You'll soon be controlling your payroll process like a pro!

Why not book a Payroll Power Hour with me? Together, we'll assess where your payroll is now, where you want it to be, and create a clear plan to get you there.

If you're looking for more in-depth support, my half-day or full-day Payroll Audit Review is the perfect next step. Together we'll dive deep into your payroll processes, identify any risks and I'll provide tailored advice to help you streamline your systems, maximise resources and enhance your employee experience. Let's make your payroll work smarter for your business.

Information on these services, as well as templates and support to help you complete the Action Points in this book, and more, are available on my website; details of which are below.

Get in Touch

I'd love to hear your payroll stories – the good, the bad and the ugly – and find out how you're getting on with controlling your payroll process, so please get in touch.
hayley@thepayrollguide.co.uk

You can find out more about The Payroll Guide through my website:
www.thepayrollguide.co.uk/the-value-of-payroll/

Connect with me on LinkedIn, as I post regular insights into payroll that you might find useful:
www.linkedin.com/in/hayleymudge

If you need a little help along your payroll journey, you know where I am.

Now go and BOSS your payroll like a PRO! You've got this!

About Hayley Paterson

Hayley Paterson is the driving force behind The Payroll Guide, her consulting brand, and Chanonry Payroll Solutions Ltd, her payroll outsourcing company. As the founder and director of both brands, Hayley is a trusted expert who delivers comprehensive payroll services to businesses across the UK, providing invaluable support to employers at every stage of their journey.

Based on the Black Isle, in the breathtaking Scottish Highlands, Hayley draws inspiration from the natural beauty of her surroundings, particularly Chanonry Point, which gave her business its name. She lives there with her husband MIchael, their son Alfie, and their dog Misty, surrounded by the tranquillity and inspiration that the Highlands provide.

Hayley founded Chanonry Payroll Solutions Ltd on 1st March 2018, shortly after welcoming her son into the world and as her maternity leave was drawing to a close. From the very start, the business had two distinct sides - outsourced payroll services and consulting - but Hayley always knew there was more potential to unlock.

By December 2024, she made the bold decision to officially split the business, giving each side the space to thrive in its own right. The consulting arm became The Payroll Guide, a brand dedicated to helping businesses navigate the complexities of payroll with confidence, while Chanonry Payroll Solutions Ltd continued to provide exceptional outsourced payroll services.

This evolution represents Hayley's commitment to excellence and her vision for the future, ensuring both brands continue to deliver the expert support UK businesses need at every stage of their employer journey.

Hayley's journey in payroll began on 31st March 2003, and since then, she has amassed a wealth of knowledge and experience. Her career has taken her through different industries, the oil and gas sector, and she's worked within multiple payroll bureaux before founding her own successful ventures. She's been involved in payrolls from a single employee to handling the complexities of a workforce of over 8,000, and Hayley wishes to share this knowledge and expertise with you. Her extensive experience means she's equipped to support businesses of all sizes and sectors.

But Hayley doesn't just love payroll, she *lives* it. She's passionate about helping employers, like you, unlock the hidden potential within payroll processes, showing that payroll doesn't have to be a source of stress and confusion that it often is for employers. With her guidance, employers can streamline their payroll operations and focus on what really matters - growing their business, safe in the knowledge that they have their payroll process firmly under control.

Hayley's mission is simple: to make payroll easier for you and to be your trusted guide through every step of your employer journey.

www.ingramcontent.com/pod-product-compliance
Ingram Content Group UK Ltd.
Pitfield, Milton Keynes, MK11 3LW, UK
UKHW021914090925
462734UK00009B/181

9 781068 447600